99 Life Lessons

99 Life Lessons

That I Learned The Hard Way

So You Don't Have To

Isaac Freed

Front Photo: Erica Tucker

Cover Design: Vanessa Mendozzi

IT Support: David Vondracek

Moral Support: Barry Cogbill

Editing & Publishing Advisor: Cynthia Martin

Author: Isaac Freed

Editor: Isaac Freed

Publisher: Isaac Freed

Copyright © 2023 Isaac Freed
All rights reserved.
ISBN-13: 978-0-9989488-2-9

Dedication

This book is dedicated to you.

I hope it has a significant positive impact on your life, and causes you to positively impact everyone whose lives you touch.

TABLE OF CONTENTS

Preface xi
Introduction xiii

PART ONE – You 1
Chapter 1   Take Care Of Yourself First 2
Chapter 2   Get Over Yourself 8
Chapter 3   Let Go 20
Chapter 4   All There Really Is To Do 25
Chapter 5   Be Quiet And Listen 28
Chapter 6   Two Ways To Make A Change 31
Chapter 7   Surround Yourself With The Right People 33

PART TWO – Your Self 35
Chapter 8   Alignment Is Mission Critical 36
Chapter 9   Never Change Who You Are To Please Someone Else 40
Chapter 10   There Are No Friends On A Powder Day 43

PART THREE – Awareness 45
Chapter 11   You Are Awareness 46
Chapter 12   Pay Very Close Attention 48
Chapter 13   Accidents Happen When Attention Lapses 52
Chapter 14   Shed Light On What Is Dark 54
Chapter 15   Look Into Your Mirrors 57

PART FOUR – Cause And Effect 61
Chapter 16   All Causes Have Effects, All Effects Have Causes 62
Chapter 17   The Power Of Belief 67
Chapter 18   You Create Your Reality And Your Reality Creates You 69
Chapter 19   Don't Force It 73
Chapter 20   Intention Is A Creative Force 77
Chapter 21   You Should Try Not To Use The Words Should And Try 79

PART FIVE – Lessons And Learning 83
Chapter 22   Always Keep Learning 84
Chapter 23   Apply What You Learn 86
Chapter 24   Life's Lessons Keep Getting Louder Until You Learn Them 88
Chapter 25   Teach Through Your Way Of Being 90
Chapter 26   Reject Other People's Limiting Beliefs 92
Chapter 27   Learn To Say I Don't Know 96
Chapter 28   Never Trust An Expert 99
Chapter 29   A Master Often Wears Plain Clothes 101
Chapter 30   Never Trust A Thin Chef Or A Fat Personal Trainer 104

PART SIX – A Few General Lessons 107
Chapter 31   If It Ain't A Hell Yes, It's A Hell No 108
Chapter 32   When You Stop Searching, It Shows Up 110
Chapter 33   Happiness Is Not An Inside Job 112
Chapter 34   Problem = Challenge = Opportunity 117

PART SEVEN – How To Live 119
Chapter 35   Be More Loving 120
Chapter 36   Chop Wood, Carry Water 122
Chapter 37   Ten Before Ten 124
Chapter 38   Have A Practice 126
Chapter 39   Practice, Practice, Practice 128
Chapter 40   How You Practice Is How You Play 130
Chapter 41   Your Life Is Your Practice 132
Chapter 42   Nothing Matters 135
Chapter 43   God Rewards Action 138
Chapter 44   Do Not Delay 140
Chapter 45   Don't Tell Me What You Can Do, Show Me 143
Chapter 46   The Value Of Self-Discipline 145
Chapter 47   Excuses Are Like Assholes 147
Chapter 48   Give Your Future Self Gifts 149
Chapter 49   Lay The Groundwork 151
Chapter 50   Honor The Process 153
Chapter 51   Finish What You Start 155
Chapter 52   Choose One Thing 157
Chapter 53   Master Something 161
Chapter 54   Be Curious 165

Table Of Contents

Chapter 55   Say Thank You 168
Chapter 56   No Bullshit. Ever 171
Chapter 57   Keep Your Agreements 174

PART EIGHT – Your Health 177
Chapter 58   Your Health Is Of Primary Importance 178
Chapter 59   Exercise Regularly 181
Chapter 60   Food Is Medicine 183
Chapter 61   The Best Drugs Are The Ones Your Body Creates 185

PART NINE – Healing 189
Chapter 62   Hurt People Hurt People 190
Chapter 63   Become Aware Of Your Traumas 193
Chapter 64   What Happened To You Is Not Your Fault, But It Is Your Responsibility 195
Chapter 65   Heal Your Wounds 197
Chapter 66   The Only Way Past Is Through 199
Chapter 67   Stay Present With Your Triggers 201
Chapter 68   Regulate Your Nervous System 205
Chapter 69   Transform Unconscious Reactivity Into Conscious Responsiveness 206
Chapter 70   The Best Healers 208

PART TEN – Other People 211
Chapter 71   The Primary Importance Of Connection 212
Chapter 72   Every Act Creates Connection Or Separation 214
Chapter 73   Find Your Tribe 217
Chapter 74   Know, Like And Trust 219
Chapter 75   Belly To Belly 221
Chapter 76   Treat Everyone With Humanness 223
Chapter 77   Don't Be An Asshole 225
Chapter 78   Never Speak Poorly Of Others 227
Chapter 79   No One Likes to Be Criticized 229
Chapter 80   You Cannot Change Other People 231
Chapter 81   Allow People To Be Exactly As They Are 233
Chapter 82   Practice Compassion From A Distance 236
Chapter 83   Personality Versus Character 238
Chapter 84   Judgment Versus Observation: It Is Okay To Measure A Man 240

Chapter 85	Be Upfront With Your Transactions	242
Chapter 86	Negotiation Versus Collaboration	245
Chapter 87	Trust Is Earned, Not Freely Given	247
Chapter 88	Trust Is Easier To Maintain Than To Repair	249
Chapter 89	Develop A Trustworthy Character	251
Chapter 90	The Value Of Validation	253
Chapter 91	Showing Up Versus Showing Off	257
Chapter 92	What's In It For Me?	260
Chapter 93	Communication Is Of Primary Importance	262
Chapter 94	Pay Attention To Non-Verbal Communication	265
Chapter 95	Pride Versus Confidence	268
Chapter 96	Grant Everyone A Wide Berth	271
Chapter 97	Stop Judging Other People	273
Chapter 98	Stop Hurting Other People	276
Chapter 99	Stop Hurting Yourself, Start Taking Care Of Yourself	277

About The Author 280
Stay Connected 282

PREFACE

For decades, I have felt something was missing from my life.

A persistent and lingering agony and despair has kept me from ever feeling content or fulfilled.

For over forty years, I have lived this way.

Discomfort can be a powerful catalyst for learning and growth.

For over a decade now, I have been collecting life lessons learned through my own search for meaning and peace, as well as from the experiences of others.

Now, I am doing my best to apply these life lessons towards living a peaceful, meaningful, empowered and enjoyable life.

The goal is to gather, remember and apply wisdom and insight, by implementing these lessons for the betterment of myself and all those whose lives I touch...

... and to share them with you.

Life is still a work in progress.

I am not perfect, or an enlightened master.

The journey is not complete.

The destination is death.

Between now and the time we die, how enriching of a life can we possibly live?

This is the question we are exploring.

Each life lesson is a piece of the puzzle that begins to answer this question.

So, let the journey begin!

INTRODUCTION

Hi, there. Thank you for picking up this copy of <u>99 Life Lessons That I Learned The Hard Way So You Don't Have To</u>.

DIFFERENT WAYS TO READ THIS BOOK

Over 1,000 life lessons were collected from 2012 to 2022, through both personal experience and the stories of others. They were then organized into a sequence so the ideas could flow from one to the next, before 99 were selected. This was a challenging task, since numerous concepts inter-relate, while others stand alone. Yet, there is a storyline to the order in which the ideas are presented. Thus, you can read this book from start to finish, and watch the big picture unfold. Often, chapters lead from one to the next. At other times, there are disjunct leaps between ideas. However, for the most part, the general message builds upon itself as the ideas flow from one to another.

A second way to use this book is to simply read the chapter titles, and imagine for yourself what each lesson means. Then, you can cross-reference your ideas with mine.

A third way to use this book is to leave it lying around, perhaps on your nightstand, coffee table or kitchen counter, and open it up randomly. Each chapter is designed to be short and self-contained, so you can absorb a single concept in one sitting, reflect upon it, and apply it throughout your day. You can read one chapter a day, one a week or one every so often.

If this book speaks strongly to you, then you can embody all its lessons. Read one chapter a week. Then spend the rest of the week applying that lesson in your life. This will take two years. Or, read two per week, and get it done in one year. Good luck!

There could be one particular life lesson that resonates powerfully with you, and you choose to focus on that. "Develop a Trustworthy Character" could be such a chapter. If you live your entire life, simply applying this one life lesson, you may be surprised how far it can take you. Or, perhaps you have already learned this one. "Master Something" could be a chapter to spend your life on. It can be your life's work to master playing the banjo or learn karate. It could be your life's work to master yourself.

ABOUT THE STYLE OF WRITING

This book is written in the style of casual conversation, as if we are familiar friends, or as if I am talking to myself.

Often, phrases and statements are repeated. There is a lyrical quality to how some ideas are conveyed, like a poem, song or casual sermon.

You will see similar concepts being repeated in multiple life lessons. One reason is that you can pick chapters to read non-sequentially without the need to remember or reference other parts of the book.

Furthermore, most of these life lessons connect to each other. There are basic concepts upon which the others are built. For instance, underlying numerous life lessons is the concept of showing up for other people, and offering the gifts of seeing and hearing them, rather than seeking validation from them. Other foundational ideas include the possibilities of becoming more self-aware and of living with integrity in relation to yourself and others. You will encounter these core principles in various forms and contexts throughout the book.

A third reason is that repetition is a key to learning.

You may notice that I almost completely avoid using the words I, me, my, mine, we, us and ours, aside from the title, this introduction, and one particular chapter. This is because you care more about yourself than you do about me. That is normal. People want to talk about themselves, and hear about themselves, not hear about me. It is not fun to engage with someone who is constantly talking about themselves. So, I have written this book speaking to you, rather than about me. In truth, it is about you, me and all of us.

In full disclosure, some lessons I have picked up from other people, while others I have learned myself. This book is a monologue to myself – "you know these things, now do them!" It is a reflection of my journey along the path of gaining an understanding of human nature, the world and myself. By reading this book, you are peering into my soul. You are reading my Notes To Self. This is the wisdom I have learned, often through pain, sometimes through joy, and sometimes from others.

Yet, it is also about you. Perhaps there are lessons here that will resonate with you and that you will find useful. These concepts are applicable to everyone. My wish is that these messages will add value to your life, and guide you towards becoming a greater version of yourself.

OPPOSITES

Every life lesson has an opposites section. For some lessons, there are no opposites. For others, there most certainly are. In fact, I do not claim to be correct about everything. These are just my and other people's observations that seem wise to apply at times. You decide for yourself if each lesson makes sense to you. Some life lessons are applicable at all times. With others, you will need to apply situational awareness and discernment to decide when they are pertinent. I am not giving you life's answers, just suggestions for you to consider and adopt, if you so choose. Do not automatically accept what I say as the truth, as if I am some infallible guru. You must think for yourself, and decide what works for you.

THE IRONY OF IT ALL

The best way to learn a life lesson is through direct experience. When you learn something "the hard way", it is more likely to stick in your brain, you are more likely to apply what you have learned, rather than if I preach it to you. Thus, it is a bit oxymoronic for me to learn life lessons the hard way, so you don't have to. Nonetheless, that is the title that came to me, so here we go.... At least some of these lessons will make sense to you, and you may realize that you have already learned them through your own experiences. The words I offer are often simple reminders of what you already know. With other lessons, perhaps I can save you a few hardships in life if you take them to heart before you have to learn them the hard way.

ONE LAST THING

If you wish to enjoy receiving one short, sweet life lesson every day, go to the website and register for 365 Life Lessons. You will get a new life lesson to contemplate every day of the year.

Whether you simply read this book, or continue your upward spiral by subscribing for your daily dose of wisdom at www.365lifelessons.com, at the very least, my sincere desire is that this book can serve you in living a fulfilling life, and enriching the lives of those you touch.

Enjoy!

Isaac Freed
November 22, 2022
www.365lifelessons.com

PART ONE

You

CHAPTER 1

Take Care Of Yourself First

This is one of the longest and most important chapters of the book. The majority of subsequent life lessons are derivatives of this one. Later chapters are devoted to specific elements of this single overarching concept.

Take care of yourself first is the progenitor lesson.

It is applicable to all areas of your life.

What does it mean to take care of yourself first?

Before looking outward, turn inward. Now, you will die before you achieve perfection, so for sure, interact with the outside world even though you are imperfect. Yet, it will serve you well to start with yourself.

Take care of yourself physically, mentally, emotionally, spiritually, and financially – as best as you can. Get your own house in order first, at least to some extent.

This life lesson is about taking full accountability for yourself and your behaviors (feelings, thoughts, words and actions), for how you treat yourself, and for how you treat other people. It covers the spectrum from taking care of your basic survival needs and your health, cleaning up after yourself, doing your inner work, becoming more self-aware, healing your emotional wounds, and on to how you show up in the world for other people. Taking care of yourself means having high integrity with yourself and others. It means knowing yourself and being in alignment with that which you truly are.

There you have it. If you stop reading right now, and take to heart the previous paragraph, you will be well on your way. Continue reading for further details:

You are the most important person in your life. People care more about themselves than others. You do too. This is natural and normal.

There is no one who will ever care about you more than you can care about yourself – aside from your mother, perhaps.

You will always be with yourself. So, care about yourself, and take care of yourself.

In fact, assume that no one cares about you, and that you are all alone in life. From this perspective, you have no choice but to take care of yourself first, foremost and fully. When you take this lesson to heart, you will always have at least one person you can count on – no matter what.

To begin:

What do air, food and sex have in common? You do not realize how much you miss them until you are not getting any.

The same can be said for your health. You do not miss it until it is gone. You take your health for granted, until you have lost it. Some folks are diligent about maintaining their health. Others, not so much. Where are you on the spectrum of self-health care, from a health fanatic on one end to severely negligent and even self-abusive on the other end? Do you prioritize taking care of your health?

> **You may take your health for granted, until it is gone. Only then might you realize what a fool you have been.**

Taking care of your health is the starting point. This is step number one. The human body has an amazing capacity not only to heal itself, but to withstand and recuperate from an extraordinary onslaught of toxins and abuse. However, the human body has its limits. No doubt, you have reached and exceeded these limits on occasion — you have lost your health at times. When you do, you remember the value of having your full natural health.

Take care of yourself, starting with your basic physical well-being. You may not fully appreciate that your body functions properly, until it does not. It is of primary importance to care for and fortify your body's health, before you begin to regret the inescapable consequences of not doing so.

Take care of your health.

On all levels.

Start by taking care of your physical health.

Without belaboring the point, a brief mention of the basics will suffice: Drink clean water. Eat healthy food. Exercise. Floss and brush your teeth every day. Practice meditation, yoga, chi gong or something similar. Sing, dance and play music. Minimize or avoid drinking alcohol, smoking, doing drugs and consuming processed foods. Get a good night's sleep.

Everything registers. Everything you do has impact. Every food you eat, every beverage you drink, is strengthening your health, or weakening it — if but imperceptibly so. Nonetheless, everything adds up over time.

> Everything registers. Everything you
> eat and drink is medicine or poison.

Part one of lesson number one cannot be over-stated: Take care of your physical health. If you do not want to take care of your physical health, then set this book down right now, and go live a mediocre, sickly and unfulfilling life.

Next, take care of your mental health.

Exercise your mind. Read books. Play music. Solve problems and puzzles. Create art. Learn new things. Have engaging conversations with other people. Meet new people! Explore new places. Keep your mind engaged, active, productive and growing. Like muscles, a mind not exercised will atrophy.

Next, take care of your emotional health.

Understand what your emotional wounds are, and seek to heal them.

Get belly to belly with people. Get to know people. Form bonds with them, and enjoy meaningful connections. Have loving relationships. Be loving and kind. Be honest and have integrity. People will want to know, like and trust you. Participate in community. Surround yourself with positive, supportive, kind and loving people. Distance yourself from toxic and negative people. Find love, be in love, make love as often as possible.

> Emotional health requires meaningful connections with other people.

Next, take care of your spiritual health.

Meditate. For at least five minutes a day, sit still, breathe, relax and notice. Notice what is inside of you – thoughts, feelings and physical sensations. Notice what is around you – sights, sounds, smells and all that comprises your external environment. Cultivate awareness and compassion, for that is your true nature. Be of service to others, for service is the highest calling. Have a practice, and practice regularly. It could be meditation, yoga, chi gong, playing the banjo, practicing karate, or any regular activity that develops the self and cultivates traits such as present moment awareness, knowledge of self and self-discipline.

Next, take care of your financial health.

Earn more than you spend (admittedly easier said than done for many folks and for many reasons). Spend less than you earn. Save up. Invest. Learn new skills so you can earn more. Ideally, have a "one-way valve", where money and other assets go in, and never come out.

Obviously, there may be obstacles to easily taking complete care of yourself on all levels. To achieve this ideal state of being may require extraordinary fortitude. Yet, learning and applying lesson number one will serve you well. So, forgive yourself for not being perfect. Then, get on with implementing these lessons as best as you can. The first step is to take care of yourself, before concerning yourself too much with the world outside of you.

Take care of your life. If you do not have food for yourself, you cannot feed other people. If you are overwhelmed by emotional pain, it may be difficult to be present and loving with others. Without your physical health, it is hard to do anything in life, really.

While some folks have their needs met by others, the message here is to not wait for anyone else, but rather to be proactive, take care of your basic human needs, then enjoy a rewarding life built on the foundation of having taken care of yourself first.

Make taking care of yourself a top priority. Make it a habit, a perpetual way of being. Every moment, every action, you are taking care of yourself — or not. Consider that, when you take care of yourself, everything else in life might just take care of itself too.

OPPOSITE

Sometimes, allow other people to take care of you. You are not alone in life. You live in an interdependent world. You are human and humans are herd animals. Working together, collaborating and helping each other is how humans survive and thrive. Someone may offer you a hot bowl of soup when you are ill, breakfast in bed on your birthday, a foot rub after a long day of work, dinner at a fine restaurant or even a cash gift. On occasion, you can let others take care of you.

Situations will arise where you may be asked to put other people's needs before your own. For example, you may have to cancel fun plans in order to help a friend in trouble. If you have children, you surely know the experience of making personal sacrifices for them. Sometimes, life requires you to put other people first.

However, although there are times when you can enjoy allowing other people to take care of you, and times when it may be wise or necessary to sacrifice your own needs and desires in service of others, as a general rule of thumb, lesson number one will serve you well, and is imperative for you to live a truly free and fulfilling life:

Take care of yourself first. Physically, mentally, emotionally, spiritually and financially, as best as you can, every single day.

CHAPTER 2

Get Over Yourself

In contrast to lesson number one, Take Care of Yourself First, which is about focusing on yourself, one meaning of Get Over Yourself is to not be self-absorbed at all.

Stop focusing on yourself, and turn your attention towards other people. Your conscious mind can only hold one thought at a time. Therefore, when you focus fully on others, you cannot be thinking of yourself. This is what it means to get over yourself. It is to give your attention to, and care about other people.

When you encounter other people, practice being totally present with them, giving them your full and undivided attention. Focus on being interested in them, rather than being interesting to them. Focus on showing up to witness them, rather than showing off to be witnessed by them. Listen attentively as they express themselves. See them and hear them, before needing to be seen and heard by them.

Showing up for other people with present-moment awareness, being genuinely interested in them, and offering them the gift of being seen and heard is an excellent way to get over yourself.

Practice this today. Be completely present with the people who cross your path, giving them one hundred percent of your attention. Then, you will not be thinking of yourself at all, and you will have succeeded in getting over yourself.

There is another meaning to the life lesson of Get Over Yourself, that is a bit trickier.

There is a dirty little secret that may need to be addressed before some folks can make a habit of getting over themselves and showing up fully for other people.

Here is another meaning of Get Over Yourself:

> To get over yourself means to be
> neither proud nor apologetic,
> neither arrogant nor humble.

Pride and shame are two sides of the same coin - insecurity. Both are symptoms of not believing that your intrinsic value has sufficient worth.

Jack Canfield said "Two out of three people have low self-esteem, look to your left and look to your right. One of you is okay, two of you are in trouble." To which Mike Smith responded, "That means one out of three people is a liar, because everyone struggles with self-esteem."

The point is that everyone falls somewhere on the spectrum of how much they believe in themselves or doubt themselves. Few people believe in themselves 100% at all times.

Put another way, psychologist Jennifer Steans has concluded, "Almost all the problems of everyone I have ever worked with come down to the same thing: The feeling of 'I'm not good enough'".

To get over yourself means to truly believe that you are good enough. Then you will be neither falsely proud nor shamefully apologetic.

Easier said than done, eh?

The belief "I'm not good enough" is held in your subconscious mind, and eradicating such self-limiting subconsciously held beliefs takes a concerted effort.

> Where do self-limiting subconsciously held
> beliefs such as "I'm not good enough" come from?

A common human experience is the wound of invalidation: betrayal, abandonment, neglect, abuse, violence, rejection and other variations on the theme of "you are not worthy of time, attention, approval, acceptance, affection or love". In other words, "you are not good enough".

Most folks experience some form of invalidation by others in their early formative years and later in life as well. Sometimes, these experiences are sufficient to program a person's subconscious mind to believe that the message "you are not good enough" is true.

> Every person has a unique temperament
> and constitution, which influences how
> they cope with the invalidation wound.

Every person has a varying degree of resiliency and experiences a varying degree of violation. Thus, given the variety of life experiences and capacities to respond, there is a wide spectrum of how you may be affected by the suggestions from the outside world that you are not good enough.

Some folks have experienced primarily supportive environments, more often receiving the message "you ARE good enough". Others are "thick skinned", and are relatively unscathed by the message "you are not good enough". For some folks, the resulting self-doubt is small. For others, the invalidation wound is deep and even debilitating. Most folks have subconsciously internalized the self-limiting belief "I'm not good enough" to some degree, be it mild or severe.

No matter where you are on the spectrum of temperament and resiliency,

> To get over yourself means to heal
> your invalidation wounds, and to reside
> in the knowingness that you are enough.

Both showing off (pride) and the fear of being seen (shame) are the results of not feeling good enough.

In his song "Only Time Will Tell" from the album "Banana Wind", Jimmy Buffett sings of his desire to find a woman of either royal or alien descent who is neither boastful nor bashful, and ponders if such a girl really exists.

Consider for yourself, are there times when you are boastful? Are there times when you are bashful?

Are these outward expressions of your subconsciously held belief that you are not good enough?

When you get over yourself, you do not feel the need to be proud or boastful in order to gain approval. You are not driven subconsciously to be validated by others. Nor are you compelled to feel ashamed of yourself or bashful, because you know you are good enough.

You can show up in the world with a quiet confidence and a peaceful presence, desiring neither to show off nor to hide away.

An example of a man who has gotten over himself is a farmer named Aaron. He grows vegetables for one of the finest, most renowned restaurants on Earth. They are beautiful to look at, delicious to eat and high in nutritional value. They are some of the most expensive vegetables in the world. Yet, when people ask him, "What do you do?" he simply replies, "I am a farmer. I grow vegetables." He does not need to impress people by telling them how important of a farmer he is. Aaron has gotten over himself, at least in this respect.

When you get over yourself, you may be a master of your craft, yet not feel the need to tell people. Your work speaks for itself. You know you are good enough, so there is no need to brag or impress people.

When you get over yourself, you will not be an attention seeker, except when appropriate, for instance, if you are an actor, musician or artist, or in an equal exchange conversation where both people take turns talking and listening.

When you get over yourself, you will stop comparing yourself to other people, concerned with whether you are better or lesser than them.

When you get over yourself, you will stop concerning yourself with what others think of you, or if they approve of you. You have the confidence and inner knowing that you are enough.

> When you get over yourself, you will stop judging other people, and allow them to be as they are.

When you get over yourself, you will be more interested in asking people about themselves – and listening – rather than talking about yourself. You will be <u>interested</u> rather than <u>interesting</u>. You will know the difference between talking <u>with</u> versus talking <u>at</u> someone. You will know the difference between false pride versus true confidence. You will understand the value of validation. You will give the gifts of seeing, hearing, witnessing and acknowledging other people, rather than seeking to receive these gifts from them.

When you get over yourself, you will find joy in being of service. To give unselfishly of yourself for the benefit of others is a form of mastery in getting over yourself.

To get over yourself is to heal your invalidation wound, and know that you are good enough.

Thus, the question arises, how can you get over yourself? How do you overcome self-doubt? How can you truly believe in yourself?

The challenge here is that the invalidation wound expresses itself as the subconsciously held belief that "I'm not good enough". Therefore, the question is:

> How can you overcome or eliminate self-limiting subconsciously held beliefs and negative self-concepts?

Is it possible to completely eradicate such beliefs, like when you pull a weed in your garden up by the roots so that it does not grow back, and is gone forever?

The author is still exploring this question, so what follows is a consideration of possibilities, rather than a definitive guide. Yet, while a comprehensive approach to overcoming self-limiting subconsciously held beliefs is beyond the scope of this book, at the same time, these life lessons are a collection of suggestions that, when applied, may help to accomplish just this.

The conundrum here is that the subconscious mind is far more powerful than the conscious mind, yet you must use your conscious mind to direct your attention, intention and actions in a manner such that you can uproot, eradicate and replace your self-limiting subconsciously held beliefs with a positive self-concept and belief in yourself.

What then, is the formula to overcome the belief that "I'm not good enough"?

First, be honest with yourself. Become aware of the extent to which you possess and are influenced by subconsciously held self-limiting beliefs such as "I'm not good enough".

Become aware of your negative self-concepts and negative self-talk, and how they impact and limit your life. Additionally, become aware of any bad habits that result from these beliefs.

Second, consider that most people never upgrade their self-concept by reprograming their subconscious beliefs about themselves. To do so requires a genuine desire, an unwavering commitment, rigorous determination and tenacious self-discipline. You must be persistent and consistent in changing not only your behaviors, but your patterns of behavior. You must abandon old habits that do not serve you, and implement new ones that do. Otherwise, you will forever return to your habituated self-concept set point, and are not likely to every reduce or eliminate self-limiting subconsciously held beliefs such as "I'm not good enough".

Searching the internet, you will discover the most common prescription for overcoming self-doubt is through the mindful application of auto-suggestion, or self-talk.

Mind what you say to yourself.

Become aware of your thoughts and self-talk. Then, notice when they reflect self-doubt. You may be surprised how often you denigrate and sabotage yourself with your inner dialogue. Once you realize how habitual this is, you may come to understand the great effort necessary to simply change what you say to yourself every day.

This is why you must be committed and persistent. It requires constant vigilance and extraordinary focus on your desired outcome. You must always be on guard against disparaging voices in your head. You must always be cancelling your thoughts and self-talk that reflect a negative self-concept, and replacing them with positive, affirming thoughts and statements indicative of a high level of belief in yourself. You must consciously and consistently choose to say kind, loving and supportive things to yourself at all times.

However, continuously monitoring your negative inner dialogue, then replacing it with a positive one, will not suffice to completely eradicate a deeply rooted negative self-concept.

Remember that the subconscious mind is vastly more powerful than the conscious mind. Therefore, mindfully and diligently applying corrective self-talk is only the first of numerous habits you must change.

What else is required? Action.
You must take deliberate, intentional, decisive, consistent and persistent action.

You turn actions into habits through consistent and persistent behavior. You must leave behind old habits, and create new habits. This is where determination, commitment and rigorous self-discipline are imperative.

Bad habits are often a reflection of a negative self-concept. Disempowering internal dialogue is one such habit. Drinking alcohol, smoking, doing drugs, eating unhealthy food, overeating, undereating, spending excessive time on social media, living a sedentary lifestyle, poor hygiene, living in a messy environment, keeping company with negative people, avoiding social interactions, spending money frivolously and needlessly accumulating possessions are examples of behaviors that can be indicative of a negative self-concept.

Good habits, such as empowering internal dialogue, sobriety, eating a healthy diet, creative self-expression, playing music, reading books, learning new things, having a practice to cultivate yourself such as meditation, yoga, chi gong or martial arts, exercising, excellent hygiene, keeping a clean environment, spending time with positive people, engaging in constructive social interactions, saving and investing money, living with only the possessions you need, truly enjoy and can afford - these are behavioral patterns that often reflect a positive self-concept.

Think about your own behaviors and habits. Which are expressions of a negative self-concept? Which indicate that you actually do believe in yourself? Most folks engage in some of each.

Consider that, by behaving in ways that demonstrate a positive self-concept, you can begin to upgrade your beliefs about yourself.

Which activities do not serve you? Which activities support you? What behaviors must you let go of and what behaviors must you adopt, so that your actions become habits, and begin to signal to your subconscious mind that you do in fact believe that you are good enough?

First comes breathing. Take a gentle, slow, even, deep inhale. Exhale the same way. Do this a few times. Make this your first new habit. Breathe fully and calmly, in and out. This will bring you to presence.

Second comes an awareness of any self-limiting subconsciously held beliefs, negative self-concepts and self-sabotaging inner dialogue.

Third comes a sincere desire to enhance your self-concept and eradicate your lingering belief that you are not good enough, or other such limiting beliefs.

You must have 100% commitment to yourself. You must take a "no matter what" approach. This will require great self-discipline. You must have courage, tenacity and grit. You must persist. You must persevere. You must be steadfastly focused on this as your goal. You must bear unwavering determination. For you must diligently unthread this subconscious belief that is woven into the fabric of your being.

> You must be committed, determined,
> self-disciplined, persistent and consistent.
> You must possess a "no matter what" attitude.

This is no easy task. This is why most people never upgrade from their familiar self-concept set point.

Have an intense and urgent desire in your soul to transform your self-limiting subconsciously held beliefs into ones that support, uplift and inspire you. Then, direct your conscious mind's attention and intention, followed by your actions, behaviors and habits, in ways that demonstrate to your subconscious mind that "I believe in myself, I am good enough".

> The more you act as if you are good
> enough, the more you will believe it.

If you are up for this challenge, then start by changing the way you speak to yourself. Make only kind, affirming statements. This requires constant vigilance and steadfast dedication. You must notice when your inner dialogue is negative, and deliberately replace your self-talk with positive words of belief and encouragement.

Next, consider your surroundings. Keep a clean environment, rather than a disorderly one. A tidy and well-ordered environment makes you feel better, and sends a message to your subconscious mind that you worthy of a clean, comfortable space.

Limit your exposure to the news, mindless entertainment and social media. This is part of having a clean, positive and supportive environment. It also frees you up to engage in activities that will boost your self-concept

You will certainly need to be careful about the company you keep. Surround yourself with positive, supportive, uplifting people. Avoid negative, pessimistic, toxic people.

Now, here is the big one:

Change your habits.

Set aside behaviors indicative of the belief that "I'm not good enough". Adopt behaviors that express the belief that "I am good enough". Make habits out of these behaviors.

Put healthy food into your body. Stop eating junk food, drinking, smoking and doing drugs, or abusing your body in any way. Start exercising, reading books and learning new things. Stop hanging out with toxic people, start hanging around positive people. Perhaps play music, sing, dance, or practice yoga, chi gong or martial arts.

Here is a little trick: Excel at what you do, and do things at which you excel. A job well done will always boost your confidence.

Another trick is to do things you love to do. When you are engaged in activities you love, you are fully present in the moment, and may find joy and peace. In these moments, you will have gotten over yourself.

The key here is to form new habits. Act consistently in ways that demonstrate to your subconscious mind that you are good enough. Initial results may come quickly, yet to completely eradicate your negative self-concept will take time, so you must be persistent and consistent.

> First, behave as if you are enough.
> Then, your underlying beliefs may
> begin to align with your actions.

This is how you apply your conscious mind to give new instructions to your subconscious mind. Habitually choose behaviors conducive to a positive self-concept, in order to uproot your self-limiting subconsciously held beliefs and replace them with a foundational self-concept that will serve you more constructively.

If you have the determination, strength and self-discipline to become aware of your self-limiting beliefs, thoughts and actions, then proceed to change them, you will begin to feed your belief that you are good enough, and starve off the belief that you are not.

Are there certain techniques that can fast-track this process?

Some folks say yes. Among the methods that can purportedly expedite the process are tapping, also known as Thought Field Therapy (TFT) or Emotional Freedom Technique (EFT), Neurolinguistic Programming (NLP), and entheogens such as psilocybin, ayahuasca or bufo alvarius. In all these instances, find qualified practitioners to work with, and understand that these techniques may or may not work for you.

One effective practice for upgrading your positive self-concept is called Cobra Breath, as taught by Master Jeffrey Boehme. One of the ultimate goals of this practice is to simply be that which you are, knowing that you are good enough. (www.cobrabreath.org)

This has been an exploration of possibilities on how to overcome self-limiting subconsciously held beliefs, so that you can Get Over Yourself. While not directly the central topic of this book, it is an underlying theme: How to relate to one's self, the world and other people in ways that promote a positive self-concept.

Self-doubt, large or small, is a hinderance to many people.

Therefore, consider the value of learning to reside in a true knowing that you are enough. Then you will live free, neither proud nor apologetic, neither arrogant nor shameful. For some folks this may easy. For others, it could be the work of a lifetime.

OPPOSITE

Sometimes, you may care about other people's opinions, for instance, in a job interview or on a first date. It is understandable if you wish to bathe, smell good, dress nicely and be liked by others.

Furthermore, humans are relational beings who have a need to feel a sense of belonging. Humans need love and approval. A performer wants their audience to applaud. Romantic partnerships thrive when appreciation and attraction are expressed. Business owners want happy customers and positive reviews. It is natural for humans to desire validation, acceptance, approval and love.

At times you will care about what other people think of you. Yet, be mindful of when this is natural and healthy, versus when it is pride or shame that is seeking approval, as an expression of an unhealed invalidation wound. Learn to recognize when your underlying motivation is the nagging feeling of "I'm not good enough".

Begin to take regular self-affirming actions, converting your behaviors into habits, thereby signal to your subconscious mind that "Yes, I am indeed good enough".

This is what it means to get over yourself.

Good luck out there!

CHAPTER 3

Let Go

Broad ranging in its meanings, to Let Go can be applied to all areas of your life.

To let go is to soften your rigidity, hold loosely your insistence that people and the world conform to your requirements, surrender your need to control everything and realize that you cannot control all aspects of your existence. Instead, go gently on your path, flow gracefully with ease, allow life to unfold naturally, allow everything to be as it is.

Easy to understand intellectually, this concept can be challenging to embody.

Give up control to a higher power. Call it God, the Universe, the Ether, Prana, the Chi Field or Cosmic Source. Allow the creative force of life to hold you, support you and guide you. Ask Source to deliver the answers to you, to show you the way, rather than doing all the work yourself. Surrender to a power, an intelligence, a force greater than you. Understand that you were created by a power greater than yourself. Know that there is an underlying intelligence or creative potential that allows life and sustains it.

If you believe in no higher power or creative source, you can simply allow everything to be exactly as it is. Surrender to the present moment, to the exact situation and circumstances of your life and the world. Stop resisting what is. There now, doesn't that feel better?

You can surrender to a higher power, or to the present moment being as it is. This is letting go, in the broader sense.

Letting go has specific applications as well.

Let go of blame and resentment to lighten your heart and free your mind. Release ill will towards others. Let people go, and you will feel peace.

Let go of beliefs that do not serve you, such as "I'm not good enough". Live unencumbered by self-doubt, free to focus on a constructive life.

Let go of all your beliefs. A belief is an adherence to an idea that cannot be proven. If you are certain of a truth, it is a knowing, not a belief. This is an important distinction. Thus, beliefs are merely probabilities. At times, believing something makes it true. At other times, your beliefs have no bearing on reality. For now, understand the difference between knowing and belief. Consider letting go of your beliefs that stand between you and freedom.

Let go of behaviors that do not serve you.

Let go of bad habits.
Replace them with good habits.

Let go of your possessions. How many are truly necessary, or bring you joy? How many are burdens, distractions and unnecessary? An extreme example is a hoarder, who collects everything. This is generally considered to be a mental illness. The lighter you live, the freer you are on all levels, physically and energetically.

Let go of lost or unrequited love so you can be present to new opportunities for connection. Of course, it takes time to heal from heartbreak. Yet, letting go of the past, you are more free to fully embrace what lies ahead. And you never know. Perhaps your most rewarding love is right around the corner.

At times, it may be wise to let go of your goals and dreams. You may think you know what you want, and go through hell to get it, only to realize it is not what you want. You may have a life path planned out, yet ignore all the signs that it is not in alignment for you. You may spend years of misery fighting an uphill battle, because you cannot let go of what is not for you. Learn to exercise discernment, so you can know when to let go.

Some folks say that rigidity is a cause of mental illness. Conversely, letting go allows for greater peace and sanity in your life.

Here is an example: You want Chinese food for dinner. Then, your friend Joe calls, and invites you to an Italian restaurant. If you join Joe for Italian food, yet spend the evening frustrated by not eating Chinese food, you will be unhappy. If you let go of your desire for Chinese food in that moment, and instead enjoy Joe's company and your Italian dinner, you are more likely to have a wonderful dining experience.

Letting go can be the difference between misery and pleasure.

If it is raining, and you get upset, let it go.

Let go of the need to control. Allow the current of the river of life to carry you.

Let go of the need to be right in arguments. Instead, seek to understand the other person. You may feel kinship, rather than isolation.

Let go of expectations, resentments and judgments. You will feel lighter and more free. Others will feel lighter and more free in relation to you.

Let go of requiring people and the world to be a certain way. Simply relax into accepting people and the world just as they are.

> Letting go is a way of being to
> practice, moment by moment,
> throughout your life. Make it a habit.
> Let go of what does not serve you.

Letting go of your desires is one of the most difficult practices in letting go. Have you ever fasted for a time? Then you know what it is like to let go of your desire to eat.

Consider what you cling to in your life, where, if you were to let it go, you would experience greater ease. Do you cling to a need for people and the world to be a certain way? Do you cling to resentments of others? Do you cling to your possessions? Do you cling to your desires?

Consider what you can let go of in your life. An excuse why you cannot do something? An old wound? A past relationship? Grief at the loss of loved ones? Shame of who you are? Judgments? Resentments? Possessions? The need for things to be different than they are?

Practice letting go right here, right now. It starts with having the self-awareness to notice that you are holding on and what you are holding on to. Then make the conscious decision to let it go. Notice something that you grasp at or resist. Now, let it go.

Make a habit out of letting things go. This requires practice, as you reroute your neural network. But you might as well get used to it, because eventually you will be forced to let everything go: your friends, family, possessions, dreams, desires and life itself.

OPPOSITE

Sometimes, you must hold on for dear life to what you truly want. It is most often with persistence, perseverance and tenacity that great things are accomplished.

Anyone who has ever become a doctor has held on tightly to their vision of becoming a doctor, until the process was complete. So too has anyone who ever built a house, or climbed a mountain. The same is true of most folks who have achieved extraordinary success or overcome seemingly insurmountable challenges.

Perhaps you are married and in conflict with your spouse. Perhaps your spouse is your best friend, and you love each other. It may be worthwhile to resolve the issues with attention, commitment and love, so you can hold on to your best friend and life partner.

Perhaps you wish to accumulate wealth and retire. Then you must secure your assets, build your net worth and hold onto your vision.

Perhaps you wish to enjoy great health. Then you cannot let yourself go physically.

Letting Go has its opposites. You must decide when to hold on, and when to let go. Situational awareness and discernment will guide you to hold on to what is important.

Let go of all the rest.

CHAPTER 4

All There Really Is To Do

All there really is to do in life is to develop compassion for all beings.

Well, okay, this is a slight overstatement. You need to secure food and shelter for yourself and possibly others. You are wise to take good care of your health. You might enjoy connection with other people and other fulfilling activities, like playing the banjo, practicing karate, swimming in the ocean, growing a garden, playing with your children, making love or whatever it is that fills you up.

All this is fine. Yet it will serve you well to learn and apply this one lesson, even if the title is slightly exaggerated.

Learn to develop compassion for all beings.

This is pretty much the purpose of incarnating into human form. Now you know the meaning of life. You are welcome.

Of course, you get to choose your own life's meanings, and these will change over time. Each day you have momentary life purposes, such as shopping for groceries or going to the gym. You may also have a single over-arching life purpose such as earning a blackbelt in karate. However, consider that there may be a greater purpose. Just maybe.

Throughout time, people have employed various means to achieve expanded states of consciousness. These include meditation, prayer, yoga, chi gong, fasting, music, dance, rigorous exercise, ingesting mind-altering substances and near-death experiences.

Under such altered states of consciousness, which some folks consider a return to a more natural state of consciousness to which modern humans have become unattuned, people often access understandings they do not see in their daily lives. A common such realization is the unity of all creation, that "we are all one", and that the ultimate truth is love.

These words are hollow on an intellectual level. When you arrive at this conclusion experientially, there is an innate knowing. You understand it without words. You embody it, at least for a moment in time. Once you have seen it, there is a part of you that always remembers.

> Whether through an altered state of consciousness, or a naturally occurring understanding, once you know, you know.

Dramatic, life-changing, consciousness-altering experiences are not necessary. Some folks simply know, naturally. Other folks are completely oblivious to this perspective. Some folks embody it all the time, in everything they do. For others, it comes and goes. Once you have encountered this knowing, either naturally or through induced means, it is always there inside of you.

However you arrive at this understanding, remember that, aside from your basic needs of survival, human connection and creative self-expression, before getting too caught up in everything else:

> All there really is to do
> in life is to develop
> compassion for all beings.

OPPOSITE

Some people believe in honoring life, yet will kill mosquitos who seek to drink their blood. They believe that self-defense is acceptable, even if you must kill someone who is attempting to kill you.

It is up to you to decide for yourself if there are exceptions to the life lesson of developing compassion for all beings.

Yet, as a general rule of thumb, this is one of the most important life lessons you can learn. It will serve you well in almost every situation. In fact, it may be one of the primary underlying reasons that you exist at all.

CHAPTER 5

Be Quiet And Listen

This life lesson is self-explanatory. It applies to most situations in your life, other than when it is required of you to speak up, or when you choose to pursue creative self-expression.

As a general rule of thumb, begin with silence and attentive listening, rather than running your mouth, running your mind, or making noise.

Start with yourself.

Listen to yourself.

Sit still, be quiet, do nothing, and listen.

Listen to your body, your mind, your heart, your emotions, your intuition.

There is a lot going on inside of you.

Become familiar with your own internal operations.

Be quiet and listen.

Some folks call this meditation, contemplation or prayer. Call it what you will, and do it. Be quiet and listen. Become calm, centered, grounded and focused. Get to know yourself.

Begin by noticing your physical sensations. Right now, see if you can feel the sensations in your hands and feet, if you are so fortunate as to have hands and feet. Now feel into other parts of your body. If you are quiet, and listen, you can feel quite a lot. When you focus on one particular body part, you might feel a buzzing sensation, or heat, or cold, for instance. No doubt, you can feel where there is bodily discomfort or pain.

Next, see if you can feel your heartbeat in your chest.

Now, can you feel into the center of your brain?

Having arrived at your brain and heart, you can start to notice your thoughts and emotions. You can observe how they arise automatically and control you unconsciously. Then you can begin to notice your reactions to stimuli, that is, to the circumstances, events and experiences of your life. How do you respond to things? Notice when you react automatically, and when you respond mindfully.

Noticing what goes on inside of you opens up a wide world of exploration and opportunity.

When you are still and quiet and listen, you can begin to notice your intuition, divine inspiration, or ideas pulled out of the ether – the infinite, timeless, formless field of source energy – whatever you wish to call it. You gain access to wisdom, insight, creativity and problem solving. You begin to listen to the signs from God, or messages from the Universe, however you care to phrase it.

You are always receiving feedback from your environments, internal and external, visible and unseen. Listen to the feedback.

First, be quiet and practice listening to yourself.

Second, be quiet and practice listening to your environment.

Third, be quiet and practice listening to other people.

When you interact with people, maintain silence and listen attentively before you speak. One of the greatest human needs is to be seen and heard, to be witnessed, validated and understood. To give the gift of time and attention, to truly see and hear another, is one of the most kind and generous acts on earth. You will enjoy connection everywhere you go, enriching the lives of all whom you encounter. In relating to others, it is a potent talent to possess and gift to offer, to be quiet and listen.

This particular meaning of this life lesson cannot be overstated. It will always, always, always serve you well to shut your mouth, and genuinely listen to other people, at least as a starting point for your interactions with them.

Shut up. Be quiet. Be still. Listen. To yourself, your body, mind, thoughts, emotions and intuition. Listen to God, Source, the Infinite. Listen to your surroundings. Listen to other people.

Be quiet and listen. Make this a habit.

OPPOSITE

There are times when you will need to do the talking. You may be the lead singer in a band, giving a presentation to a group, making a sales pitch, or asking someone on a date. You may wish to denounce an injustice, warn of danger, preach your truth or celebrate your achievements.

You will wish to connect with other people in a mutually agreeable manner, which requires two-way dialogue. In healthy relationships, be they professional, personal, or romantic, both people take time to talk and time to listen. There is an equal energy exchange.

With situational awareness and discernment, you will know when these times arise, when it is your time to talk and when to listen.

The rest of the time, be quiet and listen.

CHAPTER 6

Two Ways To Make A Change

If you want to make a positive change in your life, you only have two choices.

You can start doing something that will serve you which you are not currently doing. Or, you can stop doing something that does not serve you that you are currently doing.

If you want to break a bad habit: Stop. Then replace it with a good habit: Start. It is that simple.

Of course, it is not really that simple. People have coping mechanisms, addictions, neuroses, neurochemical dependencies, habituated neural networks, and other factors that make changing habits difficult.

Yet, it really is that simple. Now, some folks are happy as they are. If this is you, that is fine. Do not change. However, other people want to upgrade their lives and improve themselves.

> If you want to change something,
> you only have two choices:
> Start or Stop.

When it comes to eliminating bad habits, it can be helpful to: 1) Choose one thing at a time, 2) Replace a bad habit with a good one, and 3) Stay focused on WHY you want to change, and the feeling of having achieved the results you desire, so you can stay committed day after day.

Choose something you want to stop, and stop it. Choose something you want to start, and start it, in place of what you have stopped.

Here is a general example: Stop doing things that make you feel bad, or do not serve you. Start doing things that make you feel good, or do serve you. Think long term here, not just immediate gratification.

Here are specific examples: If you want to stop smoking and start exercising, every time you go for a cigarette, instead do a few situps, pushups and jumping jacks. If you want to stop eating junk food and start eating healthy, every time you go for a dessert, instead eat a mango or a carrot. If you want to stop your self-sabotaging internal dialogue, catch yourself automatically saying denigrating words in your mind, and deliberately replace them with kind messages.

Set your intention now. Choose one thing to stop, and one to start. What are they? Now, get on with it, today, tomorrow and every day!

OPPOSITE

Another way to make a change is to do more of something or less of something that you are already doing. However, this is not so much an opposite as it is a variation on a theme. You are starting to do more or stopping doing as much.

Therefore, there are no opposites to this life lesson that will serve you well.

If you want to make a change in your life, start or stop.

These are your only choices.

Otherwise, accept that you are not your ideal self, and go on being exactly as you are.

CHAPTER 7

Surround Yourself With The Right People

Your environment affects you. This includes the company you keep.

If you frequently hang out with people who drink and do drugs, you will probably find yourself drinking and doing drugs.

If you frequently hang out with people who love to barbecue chicken, you will probably find yourself eating barbecued chicken.

If you hang out with people who are kind, loving and optimistic, you are likely to be more kind, loving and optimistic than if you hang out with people who are cold hearted, cruel and pessimistic.

Surround yourself with people who are accepting, supportive, uplifting and encouraging. People who not only talk about themselves, but ask you about yourself. People who care about you. People who will help you out when you need help, and who you will want to help out too.

You will most likely become a little bit more like the people you habitually surround yourself with, so choose your friends wisely.

OPPOSITE

It is better to be alone than with people who drag you down. However, you may not be able to completely avoid toxic people, such as in a work or family environment.

At other times, exposure to diversity can expand your perspective, opening you up to new worldviews, possibilities and life experiences.

Thus, it may be impractical or unwise to only surround yourself with people who are just like you. Yet, always be mindful that your environment has an effect upon you. Thus, this life lesson has no opposite: Surround yourself with the right people

PART TWO

Your Self

CHAPTER 8

Alignment Is Mission Critical

Come into alignment with yourself. As soon as possible. As often as possible. As fully as possible.

Do whatever it takes. Make it a top priority. This is one of the most important lessons you can learn and implement in your life.

Be that which you are. As completely, as authentically and as often as you possibly can. This is an ongoing practice, not a one-time event.

Life will always send you challenges to throw you off center, to knock you out of alignment.

Stress, anxiety, worry, doubt, social pressures, the desire for approval, the need to fit in, parental expectations or rejection, judgments and demands of others, the desire for a date or interview to go well, work that you neither enjoy nor excel at, intoxicants, a partner who wants to change you…. These are examples of forces that can tempt you to be something other than that which you truly are, thus drawing you out of alignment with your real and authentic self.

To be in alignment is to be in tune with your true nature, your authentic self. Inauthenticity stems from the belief "I am not good enough". Attempting to be something you are not, in order to become good enough, is a bottomless pit that can never be filled.

Be on guard against anything that may influence you to stray from alignment with the true nature of your being.

This is a regular practice to implement in your life. Return again and again to your center, to who you truly are.

It is of the utmost importance in your life to come into alignment with the unique and everlasting truth of who you are.

When you are aligned with your true nature, your work, recreation and relationships may also be aligned with who you are — although your experiences will often test you.

> Every human being is unique,
> and so are you. It is mission critical
> for you to BE that which you are.

You have a blueprint specific to only you. Consider that, within the first molecule of a raccoon embryo, is the genetic blueprint of a raccoon. It will never become a goat or a monkey. It can only, always and ever become a raccoon.

The same is true for you.

The conditions in which that raccoon grows may cause it to be weak and unhealthy. Or, with favorable conditions and care, the raccoon may be more fully self-expressed and beautiful.

The same is true for you.

Start by acknowledging that you have a unique essential blueprint. Continue by tuning in to this blueprint of who and what you truly are. Become deeply familiar with yourself. Here, it is of great value to be quiet and listen — to your inner being.

The importance of self-awareness and self-knowledge cannot be overstated. It is imperative to realize and accept who and what you are and are not. This is mission-critical.

Become aware of your essential nature. Then, become aware of the forces that will act to knock you off your center.

Follow up this awareness with a commitment to aligning with your true nature, and not swaying from your truth.

> You must stand firmly and unshakably grounded in the truth of who you are.

Read that again. Now, say this out loud:

> "I am firmly and unshakably grounded in the truth of who I am."

For some folks this is easy. For others, not so much.

How can you come into alignment with your true nature?

Discover your true nature. Practices such as meditation, prayer, yoga, chi gong, studying wisdom teachings, entheogens, extreme sports, music, dance and ice baths are examples of methods people use to bring themselves into a present-moment-oriented, natural state of being.

Another approach to aligning with your true nature is to answer these questions: What do you love to do? What do you naturally excel at? What brings you joy? Are there activities that, when you engage in them, you lose all sense of time and self? Do these things. Your soul knows who you are, and naturally gravitates towards that which fulfills you, if you allow it to.

Take these questions seriously. Answer them repeatedly. Perhaps sleep on them overnight, allowing your subconscious mind to find the answers. The more clear you are, the greater your alignment can be.

Continuing with your self-assessment, ask yourself: To what degree are you already in alignment? What throws you out of alignment? How can you become more aligned?

What is your mission? To live your best life? To escape the pain of the presence of being? To spend a week at the beach? To send your children to college? To learn the banjo? To earn a black belt in karate?

Within your life, you will have countless missions that will change over time, and perhaps some over-arching missions as well. No matter the mission, alignment is always mission-critical.

Come into alignment with your true and authentic nature as soon as possible, as fully as possible, as often as possible.

OPPOSITE

There is absolutely no opposite to this life lesson that will ever serve you well. Alignment is mission critical.

CHAPTER 9

Never Change Who You Are To Please Someone Else

There are numerous external factors that can sway people away from their true natures.

A parent may reject a child, subtly if not outright, or in romance, one partner may seek to change the other, or people may feel pressure to conform to social norms. For instance, consider the marketing efforts exerted to encourage people to behave in certain ways.

From social influences to personal relationships, there are persistent forces that can cause people to be something other than that which they truly are.

Do not succumb to these pressures.

Be firmly and unshakably grounded in the truth of who you are.

It is a common, if not universal human need to receive approval and love. Everyone wants to belong, to be part of a group and to be accepted for who they are.

It is a common human behavior for one person to reject another person, because the other is not who the one wishes them to be. You may seek to change others so they are more to your liking. You may seek to change yourself, to be more liked by others.

For some, it can be an ever-present temptation to change who you are to fit in, gain acceptance and please other people.

Do not succumb to these temptations.

Be firmly and unshakably grounded in the truth of who you are.

While it is wise to change your undesirable traits and to become a better version of yourself, it is also wise to become aware of when you are changing who you are to please someone else.

> Notice when you behave
> inauthentically in order to
> gain approval and acceptance.

Do not change yourself to please other people.

Be firmly and unshakably grounded in the truth of who you are.

The temporary and superficial pleasure of being accepted and fitting in will be outlasted by the cognitive dissonance of not being that which you truly are. Do you know anyone for whom it has worked out well to change who they were to please another?

A corollary to this life lesson is to allow others to be who they are. More on that later.

For starters, become aware of when you may be acting like someone or something that you are not. Realize that, underneath this behavior is a need for acceptance coupled with the belief that "I'm not good enough".

Align with your true nature, know that you are enough, and you will find people who accept and appreciate you as you are. This is a far more enjoyable and fulfilling way to experience life than to seek approval artificially. When you are in alignment, you will find your tribe. You will feel far better than when you are attempting to be something other than you are.

Within you lies the blueprint of your unique and essential nature. You can never really be anything else. This is why alignment is mission critical. Come into full alignment with the true nature of your being, as soon as possible, as often as possible, as completely as possible. This is key to living a life of grace and ease, peace and fulfillment.

Be firmly and unshakeable grounded in the truth of who you are. Let nothing and no one throw you off your center.

Never change who you are to please someone else.

OPPOSITE

You may need to sacrifice some of your uniqueness to participate in society. To have a coherent social order, members must conform to societal norms – at least to some extent.

You may desire to have sex with minors. Ample evidence suggests that this is a naturally arising desire within humanity. However, society disallows this behavior, understanding that it is a severely cruel and traumatic way to treat children. Everyone involved will be better off if you refrain from full self-expression in such an instance.

Similarly, all-encompassing human nature includes a murderous side. However, you will be wise to limit the expression of such tendencies to highly appropriate situations.

With situational awareness, discernment and a bit of compassion, you can easily determine when it is wise to change who you are in order to successfully participate in society and not cause harm to others, and when it is wise to not change who you are in an attempt to gain the approval and acceptance of others.

In general, make a practice of noticing when you are inclined towards behaving inauthentically in order to receive external validation. Mitigate this tendency with a steadfast commitment to being that which you are.

CHAPTER 10

There Are No Friends On A Powder Day

The term "there are no friends on a powder day" refers to a day of skiing or snowboarding. True friends understand that the joy of skiing freshly fallen powdery snow is an exhilarating, transcendental and euphoric experience. They understand that the opportunity to ski "fresh powder" may rarely present itself, and thus, the moment is to be fully seized and exploited to its maximum potential.

If your friends ski faster than you, do not expect them to wait for you, and they will grant you the same freedom. Real friends allow each other to ski as many fresh tracks as possible, and meet up in the lodge at sunset for a hot chocolate by the fire place, resuming their togetherness only after the maximum amount of fresh powder has been skied for the day.

Real friends do not hold each other back. Real friends say, "Go for it!" "Be you!" "Maximize your joy in life!" Real friends do not demand that you sacrifice your greatest joys for them.

Do not allow others to demand that you sacrifice your joy to please them. Do not allow others to hold you back. Do not hold others back, but rather, encourage them to live their greatest lives.

If someone holds you back from pursuing your Powder Day, whatever that is for you, then they are not your true friend.

Be unapologetically and uncompromisingly that which you are. Follow your truth, pursue your dreams, and keep company only with those who want you to be happy, fully self-expressed, and fulfilled.

When people seek to change you, throw you off your center, or hold you back in life, stand firmly and unshakably grounded in the truth of who you are.

Those who seek to hold you back in life are not your allies. Surround yourself with people who support and encourage you.

Be an ally to others by uplifting rather than suppressing them. Encourage them to seize the moments of life, and set them free.

Always remember, a true friend knows that there are no friends on a powder day.

OPPOSITE

Most parents know the experience of making sacrifices for their children. Most people know the experience of making sacrifices for their partners, parents, friends or even for strangers less fortunate than themselves.

There are times when it may be appropriate to put the needs of others before your own. When you do, do so mindfully, deliberately and with good will in your heart. However, do not make a habit out of sacrificing who you are to please others. Take care of yourself first. Do not allow others to sabotage your joy or hold you back in life.

Always remember, your true friends and allies know and respect the fact that there are no friends on a powder day. Never allow anyone to discourage you, suppress you or hold you back in life, and never do so to others.

PART THREE

Awareness

CHAPTER 11

You Are Awareness

When you can step back from engaging in life, quiet your mind and listen, you may begin to observe yourself. Notice your physical sensations, thoughts and emotions. Notice how you respond to the condition of being alive. How do you respond to the circumstances, events and people you encounter?

Who, or what, exactly, is doing the noticing? There is a part of you that is experiencing your sensations, thoughts and feelings. There is another part of you, more subtle, that is realizing that you are having these experiences.

Some folks call this The Witness, when you can stand back and observe yourself. They then ask who or what is it, that is doing the observing? The answer they arrive at is that it is a conscious Awareness. Some folks say this conscious Awareness precedes the physical self. They have concluded that there is a primary unified field of Awareness underlying all creation. Do you believe this may be true?

Consider the possibility that:

All externally constructed layers of self aside, at the very core of your being, resides a conscious Awareness.

Think about your outer identity. You may call yourself a doctor, lawyer, carpenter, accountant, entrepreneur, musician, painter, fisherman or gardener. Perhaps you call yourself a karate fighter or banjo player. You may say that you are kind, generous, wise or wealthy. You may describe yourself in many ways, and indeed, you may possess all these attributes.

These are the layers of who you are on top of your core essence.

What is underneath these outward definitions? Peel away the layers of how you define yourself in making money, in relationships, in creative expression, in leisure and recreation, in what you do and how you behave in life. What remains? You are a body, comprised of flesh, blood, bones, organs, lymph, nerves and so on. But are you just a mechanical meat suit with chemical reactions and electrical impulses? Or is there something more?

Scientists can identify where cognitive functions occur within the brain. However, they cannot localize consciousness itself. Consciousness appears to be everywhere, not reliant upon time, space or the contents inside your physical head.

Is there a consciousness that underlies and permeates all of creation?

In remote viewing experiments, subjects were often able to accurately determine the secret locations of hidden objects, sometimes before the decisions were made where to hide them. Consciousnesses can access information beyond the confines of location or linear time.

Consciousness seems to be everywhere, all at once. Is it the foundation for everything? Consider that, all externally constructed layers of self aside, at the core of your being, you are Awareness.

OPPOSITE

Some folks might argue against the hypothesis that you are Awareness. They could point out that people are often unconscious, or that science has not proven the theory of One Great Mind. They might disagree that there always resides a fundamental Awareness at your core. The precise nature of your fundamental self may be impossible to prove. However, consider that, on a practical level, you are always somewhere along the spectrum between completely unaware and pure Awareness. On a foundational level, it could be that you are Awareness itself.

CHAPTER 12

Pay Very Close Attention

This life lesson applies to all aspects of your existence. Every experience, every person, every moment of life itself.

In every moment there are more stimuli coming your way than you can possibly register on a conscious level. Furthermore, it is difficult, if not impossible, to always be paying perfect attention.

Nonetheless, while maintaining 100% pure present moment awareness at all times is next to impossible, simply remember, as often as possible, to pay attention as best as you can. Move up the spectrum of presence, towards greater attunement with your inner and outer worlds.

The concept is simple. The application requires intention and will.

As a general rule of thumb, it will always serve you well to pay very close attention to what is happening inside of you, and all around you.

Here are specific examples to guide you:

Start by paying attention to yourself:

Physically, what is going on with you? How do you feel? How does it feel inside of your body? Your hands and fingers? Your feet and toes? Your arms and legs? Your belly and chest? Can you feel your heartbeat? Where are you tense? Where are you relaxed?

Pay attention to your body.

Pay attention to your posture and body language. What are you expressing by how you carry yourself?

Pay attention to your breath. Are you a chest breather, or a belly breather? Are you taking slow, relaxed, deep breaths, or short agitated ones? Take a long, deep, gentle, even inhale. Hold for a moment, then exhale gently, slowly, evenly and completely.

Next, pay attention to your mind. Notice your thoughts. Are they positive or negative? Constructive or not? Do you allow your thoughts to direct you? Or do you direct them? Probably, some of each.

Next, pay attention to your emotions. How do you feel? Are you on track or is something upsetting you? Do you need to address an issue, or are you doing just fine? What are your emotions telling you?

Can you pay attention to your intuition? If so, what does it say? Be quiet and listen, allow your intuition to guide you as no mental process can.

Next, pay attention to your actions. What are your behaviors, habits, reactions, distractions and addictions? What are your good habits that support your health, happiness, prosperity and well-being? What are your bad habits of self-sabotage and escapism?

Next, pay attention to your surroundings. Listen to the songs of the birds. Witness the beauty of flowers in bloom. Sense the sun on your skin. Feel the rhythm of rain hitting the roof. Tune in to the symphony of the sounds on the street. Notice your environment.

Next, pay attention to other people.

Pay attention to people's subtle energies. What do their facial expressions, posture and body language say? Are they present and grounded, or lost in the clouds? Are they happy or sad, peaceful or agitated? Pay attention to the texture of their eye contact, or lack thereof, and the firmness of their handshake or hug. Pay attention to what they say, and how they say it. What is the nature of their characters? What is the texture of their hearts? Are they respectful, considerate and trustworthy, or not so much?

Pay attention when you interact with other people. How do they impact you? How do you respond to them? What is your impact upon them? How do they respond to you?

How do you relate to other people? Are you distant, closed off and protective? Or are you warm, open and curious? Are you judging them? Do you think you are better or lesser than them? Are you vying for their attention and approval? Or are you present with them, seeing, listening to and acknowledging them?

If you have a partner, pay attention to your partner. Pay attention to their needs and desires. Listen to the words they speak. Notice how they feel. Notice how their body responds to your touch. Pay attention to everything about them. To not do so is abusive.

If you have children, pay attention to them. Children thrive like flowers in high quality soil with sunlight and water, when they are given time and attention. They develop emotional problems and mental illness without them.

Pay attention to other people. Offering your time and attention to another is one of the greatest gifts you can give.

Practice paying attention. Clear your mind and become calm. Sit still for five minutes. Do nothing other than paying attention to your breath. Notice when your mind wanders and bring it back to your breath. This is the first practice to cultivate your ability to pay attention.

Pay attention to yourself – physically, mentally and emotionally. Pay attention to your behaviors – the ones that support you and the ones that do not. Pay attention to what you are doing, thinking and feeling in each moment, as often as possible. Pay attention to how you interact with and respond to the world around you.

Pay attention to your environment and surroundings.

Pay attention to other people.

Pay attention to your loved ones. Pay attention to your partner to deepen connection and express love. Pay attention to your children. Children require attuned parenting to become emotionally healthy, well-adjusted human beings. All relationships require attuned relating for them to flourish.

> Paying attention is a practice,
> moment by moment, to
> cultivate throughout your life.

Practice paying attention.

Pay very close attention.

OPPOSITE

Sometimes it is nice to just rest. But be careful! It can become a habit to always be occupied, always distracting yourself from unpleasant feelings or never fully present. Give yourself a break from paying attention, if you need to.

However, as a general rule of thumb, it will serve you will to pay very close attention to all areas of your life, as often as possible.

CHAPTER 13

Accidents Happen When Attention Lapses

Have you ever noticed that when you have an accident or make a mistake, it was usually in a moment of inattention?

When you stub your toe, spill a beverage, trip and fall, break something or crash a car – you are generally not paying attention. If but for a moment in time, your awareness has faltered.

When you make a mistake, it occurs because you miss a moment in time. You mind has wandered from the task at hand.

Thus, paying attention helps you avoid accidents and mistakes that are annoying or expensive at the least, severe or fatal at the worst.

This lesson holds true not only for physical injuries and property damage, but for human relationships as well. In relation to others, everything you do creates connection or separation. When you say something hurtful or unwise, it causes conflict and creates separation. Usually, such moments occur during a lapse of awareness.

In particular, when a person's unhealed wounds get triggered, they tend to react automatically from a place of unconsciousness to disrupt or destroy the connection in the relationship. More on this later.

By paying attention, you can minimize your exposure to the risks of physical injury, property damage and sabotaging your interpersonal relationships.

Here is another reason to pay close attention:

To be seen and heard is one of the greatest human needs. To truly see and hear another is one of the kindest and most generous gifts you can possibly give. To not see or hear another is one of the cruelest abuses. By paying attention to the people in your life, you will cultivate connection and loving relationships. By not paying attention to the people in your life, you will, by definition, be abusing them, and you may find yourself very lonely. This is a grave mistake you are hereby well advised not to make.

To always be 100% present is a challenging, if not impossible ideal. However, it will serve you well to increase your ability to remain present.

The more you are present with yourself, others and the world, the more you can avoid accidents and mistakes that will be costly and painful.

Why? Because accidents happen when attention lapses.

OPPOSITE

There is no opposite to this life lesson that will ever serve you well. Accidents happen when attention lapses. So pay attention.

CHAPTER 14

Shed Light On What Is Dark

"One does not become enlightened by imagining figures of light, but by making the darkness conscious." - Carl G. Jung

Most, if not all people, have blind spots. Even the Dalai Lama, who was a vegetarian, was told by his doctors that he needed to start eating meat. If the spiritual leader of Tibetan Buddhism has blind spots, you probably do too.

By definition, you cannot see your own blind spots.

You can, however, increase your self-awareness by discovering aspects of yourself about which you are currently unaware. Seek to shed light on what is in the dark.

Methods to achieve this include, amongst others, contemplation, self-inquiry, a meditative or spiritual practice, studying with a teacher or mentor, the use of entheogens, and conscious relationships.

To seriously go deep, ask your friends and family how they see you. It may feel awkward, yet can be quite revealing. Hopefully, they will be honest.

Perhaps you are stingy, but think you are generous. Perhaps you are easily angered, but see yourself as calm and non-reactionary. Perhaps you are a co-dependent people pleaser, but believe you are confident and strong.

This lesson is a corollary to many others. You are Awareness, so become more aware of yourself. Alignment is mission critical, so align with your true nature by knowing who and what you truly are. Take care of yourself first – before pointing out other people's faults, shortcomings and blind spots, discover your own.

Other lessons are corollaries to this one. Upcoming lessons in this book address your big blind spot: become aware of your traumas, become aware of your triggers, regulate your nervous system so you can stay present with your triggers, then transform unconscious reactivity into conscious responsiveness. This can be the difference between broken relationships and broken hearts versus a peaceful, connected and fulfilling existence.

There is a creation myth that all the Universe is but a singular consciousness that has fragmented itself for the purpose of getting to know itself better. In this case, discovering who you are, including your blind spots, is the reason why you exist. Decide for yourself if you want to adopt this possibility as a consideration or guiding principle.

Nonetheless, it is a worthwhile lesson to implement in this lifetime: Shed light on what is dark – become aware of your blind spots.

In particular, discovering your blind spots can improve your human relationships, bringing more connection, fulfillment and joy, because you will be less likely to behave unconsciously in ways that create separation.

OPPOSITE

Do you ever hang out with people who are always applying self-inquiry or spiritual teachings to their lives? They may always be seeking to frame every action as masculine or feminine, sacred or profane. It gets exhausting.

Sometimes, the most spiritual and "awake" people are the ones who are just going about living their lives, and being decent human beings, while the folks striving for perpetual self-improvement sound like broken records from the latest trending spiritual guru's tropical retreat.

Sometimes it can be refreshing to take a pause from self-discovery and personal growth work. Just go about life being who you are, doing what you do, without the need to constantly analyze everything. Eat some tacos, drink a cold beer, dance to your favorite music, and let go of your thinking mind.

Nonetheless, throughout your lifetime, it is a good idea to increase your self-awareness from time to time.

Therefore, there is no opposite to this life lesson, other than to take an occasional break from perpetually doing your inner work.

As a general rule of thumb, it will serve you well to shed light on what is dark. Get to know your blind spots. The sooner the better.

CHAPTER 15

Look Into Your Mirrors

Consider the possibility that:

Everyone you encounter is a reflection of you. What you like or dislike about others is a reflection of what you like or dislike about yourself.

To learn what you do not know about yourself, recognize each person as your mirror, reflecting back to you an aspect of yourself. Consider both the positive and negative traits a person demonstrates.

Some folks are more neutral as mirrors than others, they may not be your stark reflections. However, it is guaranteed that others will prominently reflect your nature back to you, especially your blind spots. You can choose to look, or not.

You can notice when another is reflecting a desirable trait you possess, such as kindness or generosity. Congratulate yourself for your positive qualities and please, practice enhancing and expressing them.

The more important - and more difficult - practice is to witness the unpleasant and undesirable aspects of your nature being reflected back to you by others. This can threaten your pride. Yet with humility, it can be a great teacher, and ultimately make you a better person. This is an advanced practice in self-awareness.

Most people are not willing to look into their mirrors, see others as reflections of themselves, shed light onto their darkness or become aware of their blind spots. To do so requires great courage, and will place you in a very small minority of humanity. You are now on your way to becoming superhuman.

> When you point your finger at someone else, remember, there are three fingers pointing back at you.

Every time you judge or criticize others, imagine how the trait or behavior you are condemning may be an aspect of yourself that you dislike, judge, deny or reject, and about which you are unaware. When you find fault with another, consider that it is an aspect of yourself being reflected back to you.

When you find yourself condemning another person for being selfish, disrespectful, inconsiderate or unwise, ask yourself if you possess these same undesirable traits.

> To look into your mirrors, you must be ruthlessly honest with yourself. You will see aspects of your character that you do not like, and that will disappoint you.

However, would you prefer to live in ignorance and denial of your true nature? Or would you prefer to know yourself?

If the answer is the latter, then take a good look in the mirror that every other person is for you. This is one of the best ways to shed light on what is dark, to increase your self-awareness and to get to know your blind spots.

A variation on this theme is that another person may not reflect back to you an exact trait that you possess, but rather may cause a trait to surface in you that is unconscious and could use attention and work. For instance, you may be such a giving person that you have weak boundaries. You may then frequently encounter others who are takers, not givers, and abuse your generosity. Perhaps you have trouble standing up for yourself, and others often take advantage of you. Perhaps you have an anger management problem, and others often enrage you. In such instances, these folks are not reflecting your exact traits back to you, but rather causing to arise within you the parts of yourself that you would do well to become aware of, address, rectify and strengthen.

Thus, when you are confronted with a difficult person or situation, ask yourself if they are directly reflecting back to you an aspect of yourself, or if they are placed before you to elicit a blind spot that they do not reflect directly, but that you are nonetheless wise to confront.

OPPOSITE

Some folks may not necessarily reflect aspects of your personality or character back to you. There is not much energetic charge between you. There is not much unresolved karma between you.

Sometimes, people are just jerks and behave inappropriately, and it has little if anything to do with you.

At other times, it can be exhausting to perpetually be doing the inner work of self-realization, so it is okay to take a break.

However, as a general rule of thumb, you will be wise to remember that others are often your mirrors and can help shed light on your blind spots.

Therefore, there is no opposite to this life lesson that will serve you well.

Look into your mirrors.

PART FOUR

Cause And Effect

CHAPTER 16

All Causes Have Effects, All Effects Have Causes

There are different opinions about the nature of cause and effect. Does anyone really know the truth? No, but you can contemplate.

Consider that:

Everything you do has an impact.

Everything registers.

Every cause has effects.

Every effect has causes.

In other words, everything you do influences the subsequent outcomes in your life and the world. No matter how small or indefinable, every input informs the outputs. Every result in your life was caused by preceding factors, at least some of which were set into motion by you.

"Everything happens for a reason" does not necessarily mean that God has a predetermined plan for you, and is forcing upon you every experience. What it means is that for each effect, or outcome in your life and in the world, there are causal factors. There are reasons (causes) why things happen (effects).

Now, consider this:

All Causes Have Effects, All Effects Have Causes

Every thought, feeling, word and action is a cause set in motion.

Everything you think, feel, say and do sends causational ripples out into the single, unified, infinite, timeless, formless field of creative potential source energy that underlies, permeates and brings forth into existence all of creation. Intention travels instantaneously throughout all time and space. (Decide for yourself if you want to believe this theory.) From this perspective, consider the wisdom of being mindful of, and deliberate in: what you think, how you feel, what you say, and what you do.

Furthermore,

You are not likely to escape the consequences of your actions.

All of your behaviors — thinking, feeling, speaking and acting, are causes that will have an effect on you and the world, sometimes obvious, sometimes subtle. Your behaviors have consequences.

You may not be able to successfully predict the outcomes of all the causes you set in motion. Indeed, every effect, or outcome, is the result of numerous, if not infinite, causal factors. Additionally, your actions may have impacts other than what you think.

Yet, understanding that all causes have effects, that all effects have causes, that everything registers, that your thoughts, feelings, words and actions are causes set in motion, and that you may not be able to escape the consequences of your actions,

You can be mindful of behaving wisely, thus setting forth causes into motion which have a favorable likelihood of producing more desirable results in your life and the world.

Some obvious examples:

If you lead a sedentary life and eat unhealthy food, do not be surprised if you become overweight or develop heart disease. Cause and effect.

If you study with a skilled banjo teacher and practice diligently, there is a high likelihood that you will become a talented banjo player yourself. Cause and effect.

Here are more fun examples:

If you get high on drugs and go pick a fight with law enforcement officers, you can guess that the effects of the causes you have set in motion are likely to be undesirable. Of course, you might become best friends with the cops, or encounter a new business partner during your time in jail. So, you do not really know the effects of the causes you have set in motion until events have played out. However, you can make a reasonably educated guess about probable outcomes.

If you eat nutritious food and exercise regularly, you can guess that you may be healthy and fit. Of course, you might break a leg while running, or choke to death while eating broccoli. So, you do not really know the effects of the causes you have set in motion, until events have played out. However, you can make a reasonably educated guess about probable outcomes.

Be mindful of what you think, feel, say and do. Everything has impact. Everything registers.

The point here is that, without diving too deeply into theoretical quantum physics, spiritual mysticism or statistical analysis, you can figure out with fair probability which behaviors in your life are wise, and which ones are not. In Buddhism this is called Wise Behavior.

Everything you do today influences the circumstances, events, and experiences that you will encounter in your future. This is especially relevant when it comes to your habitual ways of being.

What are the habits of your mind? Do you speak to yourself with kindness, confidence and encouragement? Or with criticism, self-doubt and disparagement? Are you thinking thoughts of approbation towards others, or of disdain? Are you fearful of what awaits you in each oncoming moment, or excited to meet it? Does your mind chart its own course, wandering aimlessly, or do you have dominion over your thoughts?

How do you habitually treat your body? Do you give it natural foods and nutrient rich calories, or processed chemicals and empty calories? Do you exercise your muscles, heart and brain, or allow them to atrophy? Do you regulate your nervous system, or let it run wild?

How do you habitually treat other people? With presence, acceptance, validation, forgiveness, benevolence and love? Or with indifference, judgment, discouragement, criticism, invalidation or scorn?

How do you habitually approach life? How are your habitual thoughts, feelings, words and actions continuously setting forth causes into motion, and what are the likely effects?

Be mindful of cause and effect. Be mindful that your behaviors are causes set in motion. They will have effects, the consequences of which may be inescapable.

What you have and experience in your life today is, at least partially, the result of past causes you have set into motion. What you do today influences the future effects that you will experience.

Good luck out there!

OPPOSITE

Sometimes, bad things happen to good people. Some folks believe that for every action, there is not necessarily an equal and opposite reaction. Perhaps events can arise randomly, without cause. Is it possible to escape the consequences of your actions? For instance, you might act in an unethical manner and harm others, yet profit handsomely.

You decide for yourself if you want to believe in cause and effect.

Whatever you choose to believe, it remains possible, if not probable, that all causes have effects, all effects have causes, everything registers, everything has an impact, all thoughts, feelings, words and actions are causes set in motion, and the consequences of your actions may be inescapable.

Thus, it is wise to be mindful of the causes you set in motion.

Therefore, there is no opposite to this life lesson that will serve you well.

Behave wisely.

CHAPTER 17

The Power Of Belief

Belief is one of the greatest forces that humans possess. It is powerfully creative.

It has been demonstrated that people can heal themselves from physical ailments using only the power of belief. This is called the placebo effect.

What this means is that you can literally rearrange the molecules that make up your physical reality with your mind.

Sit with this fact for a moment. Get a firm grasp on this concept.

What you believe can be greater than objective "reality".

Perhaps you are a talented person, but believe you are not. This self-limiting belief will keep you from fully expressing your talents. Perhaps you are surround by people who love you, but you do not believe you are loveable. This self-limiting belief will keep you from fully receiving the love that is available to you.

Conversely, perhaps you are a fairly average person. Yet you firmly and fully believe you are destined for greatness. You will most likely achieve greatness.

Take note of your beliefs about yourself. Honestly take stock of your self-concept. Shed light on your blind spots. This requires delving into the dark recesses of your subconscious mind. Your deeply ingrained subconsciously held beliefs about yourself inform every aspect of your life, whether you are aware of them or not.

> Your beliefs about yourself are the limiting factors in your life. They can also be the liberating forces.

What are your beliefs about your physical appearance? What are your beliefs about your inner beauty? What are your beliefs about how competent and capable you are? What are your beliefs about how worthy of love and acceptance you are? How do your beliefs about yourself impact your reality? How do they limit you – or set you free?

Your beliefs create your life. This is the power of belief.

Understand the power of beliefs. Become aware of your beliefs and how they serve you or wreck you. Remember, when you hold a belief strongly enough, it will rearrange the molecular structure of your physical realty.

OPPOSITE

Sometimes, your beliefs have no power. If you walk outside while it is raining, believing you will not get wet, your belief is inconsequential. You will get wet. Sometimes, the world simply is the way it is.

Herein lies the great conundrum. At times, your beliefs can alter the molecular structure of physical reality, as proven by the placebo effect. At other times, they are powerless against the greater reality in which you exist.

Nonetheless, it will always serve you well to remember how powerful beliefs can be. For example, your self-concept can be a self-fulfilling prophecy. Being mindful of this, you can cultivate beliefs about yourself that will rearrange physical creation in your favor.

CHAPTER 18

You Create Your Reality AND Your Reality Creates You

There is a modern personal empowerment teaching that you are 100% responsible for creating everything in your life, through your thoughts, feelings, words, actions and vibrational frequencies. There are folks who preach this 100% theory as if it were a fact, but it is only a theory.

There is merit to the idea that the frequencies at which you are vibrating may be attracting into your life resonant frequencies and repelling dissonant ones.

However, it seems likely that the frequencies, energies, people, events and circumstances surrounding you also have an impact upon you.

Cause and effect is a two-way street. You create your reality – to an extent. The greater reality in which you exist also creates you.

For instance, folks who profess this 100% theory tend to fall short of demonstrating their ability to craft a reality precisely as they wish it to be. Furthermore, consider the innocent victims of abuse, violence and war. Do you really think such people categorically call such experiences into their lives due to their inner states of being?

Going deeper still, understand that, your mother was born with all of her eggs inside of her, including the one that became you. All of the conditions surrounding her conception, gestation, birth and formative years began to impact the very nature of your being, long before you were born or named. You will be wise to understand the genetic, familial and transgenerational forces that have shaped you. While it may be that you have the free will to choose how to respond to the circumstances of your existence, it is certain that you have been shaped by external influences such as these.

There are infinite external forces perpetually influencing you.

Perhaps on some mystical, spiritual, theoretical quantum physics level, the 100% theory is true: Perhaps your soul chose to incarnate in your physical form this lifetime to learn from your particular experiences, including the ones that appear horrible to the human eye. Furthermore, if everything in existence is an expression of a singular unified field of consciousness, from which all arises and to which all returns, then yes, everyone else is you and you are everyone else. Thus, this all-encompassing source consciousness – which is you – creates absolutely everything. But these are merely possibilities to be considered, not incontrovertible truths

On a practical, day-to-day level, in this physical world of duality, linear timelines, separation from source, birth, life, death and limited consciousness, this 100% theory is misleading, if not false. Your surrounding environment also has an impact upon you. The interplay of cause and effect between you and the Universe goes both ways.

> This does not justify victimhood
> of forces beyond your control,
> or abdication of responsibility
> for being at cause in your life.

Indeed, you do create your own reality, in part. Remember, your thoughts, feelings, words and actions are causes set in motion, and all causes have effects.

Furthermore, your beliefs alone can rearrange the molecular structure of your physical reality, as demonstrated by the placebo effect.

But the placebo effect does not work all of the time. You cannot control ALL of your reality.

This piece of the puzzle is missing from the 100% theory, leaving people attached to a lopsided and disorienting belief system, bewildered and ashamed when they cannot control the entirety of their existence.

By all means, strive to create for yourself the life you desire. Emit positive vibrations, focus on your goals, and submerse yourself in the feeling state of already having achieved them. There may be power in these practices. Yet, it will serve you well to acknowledge, understand and accept the fact that some things are beyond your control. There are outside forces that affect you, no matter your efforts to "manifest" reality.

Be aware of the external influences that have an impact upon your life and state of being.

Take into account how your environment affects you. Do you live in a bustling city or peaceful rural area? Where you live impacts your state of being. Is your home clean and tidy, or cluttered and disorganized? The orderliness of your home, or lack thereof, impacts you.

Now, consider the company you keep. Are the people around you pessimistic, judgmental, criticizing and complaining? Or are they optimistic, accepting, encouraging and grateful? You are always being influenced by the people in your life.

Your surrounding environment is always impacting you, thus the importance of keeping a clean environment and surrounding yourself with the right people.

Be aware of how your environment impacts you, so you can choose environments that impact you in ways that you prefer.

Now consider the ways in which you impact other people. Consider how you interact with other people. Are you present and attentive when they speak to you and express themselves? Or are you checking your phone or scanning the room for more interesting or attractive people? Are you listening to respond or to understand? Are you supportive and encouraging, or critical and discouraging? How do you impact other people? No matter your way of being, you are always impacting those with whom you interact, and they are impacting you.

You create your reality, and your reality creates you. There is a constant interplay of internal and external forces exchanging information. You can choose to be mindful of, and deliberate in the creation of your reality. Likewise, you can be mindful of how your reality creates you, and seek to find yourself in supportive environments.

OPPOSITE

Is it possible to move through life without being impacted by the world around you? Is it possible that you and you alone are 100% responsible for creating your entire reality? Conversely, is it possible to have zero impact on others and the world? Or is it more likely that your internal state of being and your external environment have an effect upon each other?

You must answer these questions for yourself.

However, it will serve you well to be mindful of the possibility that you impact your environment, and external forces impact you.

CHAPTER 19

Don't Force It

This life lesson can be applied to all areas of your life – at times.

Some folks get carried away with the idea that they create their own reality, and they seek to bend the world to their will. This is not inherently a bad idea. If you wish to negotiate a low price for the car you are buying, get a date with a person you like, learn to play the banjo, earn a black belt in karate, speak a foreign language or build a house, then go for it! You can have a desire, set an intention, take action, and create the reality you want – to an extent.

However, you may begin to strive excessively towards achieving your goals and desires in a way that is contrived, not in alignment with the true nature of your being, and contrary to the will of the world. This is called forcing it.

There is another way to live. It is called going with the flow, or allowing. Surrender to a wisdom that is beyond you, God, the Universe, your higher self, Prana, the Ether, the Chi Field, whichever is your preferred creative force that brought you forth into existence. Perhaps it is more powerful than you are. You can set intentions, but hold them loosely. Trust that the creative forces of life will send you off in the direction you need to travel. This is allowing, rather than forcing.

Sometimes, you need to take decisive action towards a desired outcome. At other times, it will serve you well to remember: Don't force it.

You may find yourself striving towards an objective, but it is not working out. You may feel unpleasant or even terrible about it. The world may be giving you signs to stop forcing it. You may be clinging to something long after it is time to move on. If you pay attention to the signals, and choose not to force it, your life may be far more graceful and easy. Do you ever find yourself fighting uphill battles that you know, deep down inside, are not the hills you want to die on?

Don't force it.

Another application of this life lesson is to simply be that which you are. Remain grounded in your authentic truth. Do not pretend to be something other than you are, in order to gain attention, acceptance or approval.

Don't force it.

If you are applying for a job that you subconsciously know you do not want, you are forcing it. If you are going on a date with someone who does not excite you, you are forcing it. If you are participating in an activity when you do not want to, you are forcing it.

If you are behaving in a way that is inauthentic to the true nature of your being, you are forcing it.

Don't force it.

Your programming and conditioning may cause you to behave inauthentically. For instance, the subconsciously held belief that "I am not good enough", coupled with the desire for love and acceptance, may cause you to force it. Become aware of when, how and why you force it, so you can stop, thus living in alignment with your true nature.

Be that which you are, even in the face of pressure to conform to social norms, the desires of others, or the need for approval.

Don't force it.

Don't force it can be applied to romantic relationships. If you want to be with someone who does not want to be with you, don't force it. If you already have a partner, and you want him or her to change, they will not. You must accept them completely as they are. You cannot force it.

Don't force it can be applied to creative endeavors. If you are writing an essay, poem or song, and feel stuck, don't force it. Go for a walk, do something else, forget about it, and come back later with a clear mind, when you can flow more easily.

Don't force it can be applied to any area of your life. Have you ever done mechanical or construction work? What happens when you turn a screw too tightly? It breaks, because you were forcing it.

To force it means to be out of alignment, to go against the flow, to go against the natural order of the world.

When you force it, significant effort is required. That is literally the definition of force. The results will generally not be as good as when you are in alignment with yourself and flow more easefully with the natural way of the world.

To what areas of your life can you apply this life lesson? Where are you forcing it unnaturally? Can you surrender, and go with the flow instead?

OPPOSITE

Sometimes, tenacity and perseverance are required if you want to achieve your dreams, or simply feed your family. There are times when you must force it. The key here is to exercise situational awareness and discernment - become aware of when it is wise to force it, and when it is not.

Consider a wildcat, lounging high up in the branches of a jungle tree. It mostly lays around doing nothing. Then, every so often, it pounces on its prey, so it can eat, and return to hanging out in the trees. The wildcat is mostly not forcing it. Every once in a while, it must use force to sustain itself. The wildcat, being in alignment with the natural order of things, only forces it when necessary.

Your practice today can be to know when to exert effort, and when to go with the natural flow of the world. Listen to your quiet, subtle inner voice. At times, you will hear it saying "Go for it!". At other times, you will hear it saying: "Don't force it."

CHAPTER 20

Intention Is A Creative Force

It has been said that energy flows where attention goes, that energy follows thought, and thought becomes matter.

Your thoughts, feelings, words and actions are causes set in motion.

All causes have effects, all effects have causes.

Much, if not all, of what has been created by humans began as thoughts.

For instance, you cannot plant a vegetable garden, build a house, or earn a black belt in karate without first intending to do so.

Every day you set and implement intentions, whether you are aware of them or not. You are always creating.

There is an intention behind pouring a bowl of cereal for breakfast. There is greater intention behind learning to play the banjo. Sometimes there is intention behind creating a child, sometimes there is not.

What you focus on grows in your life. If you often think about how humans are stupid and cruel, you will find examples to support your thesis. Conversely, if you often think about how humans are intelligent and kind, you will find examples to support this conclusion as well.

Thoughts become things, they say.

"We become what we think about," said Earl Nightingale. "Whether you think you can, or think you can't, you're right," said Henry Ford.

You are not likely to create much of anything substantial in this world, unless you intend to do so first and believe that you can.

You are always emitting your intentions into the great cosmic soup, whether you are aware of it or not. You are always setting forth causes into motion. Be mindful of what you are sending out. Be clear and deliberate with your intentions.

Direct your attention and intention towards what is important to you.

What are your intentions in your life? What are you creating?

Remember, intention is a creative force, and you are always creating.

OPPOSITE

Amongst certain circles, it is still open for debate as to whether the Universe was created intentionally or accidentally, has a point of origin, or has existed forever. Is there intention behind every act of creation?

Albert Hoffman discovered the psychedelic properties of LSD accidentally. Alexander Fleming invented Penicillin accidentally. The author of this book was conceived accidentally.

Sometimes situations and experiences arise seemingly without purposeful causation. Intention may not be required for creation.

Yet, it remains that intention is a creative force. Therefore, there is no opposite to this life lesson that will serve you well. Be mindful of your intentions and deliberate in setting them.

CHAPTER 21

You Should Try Not To Use The Words Should and Try

In accordance with the life lessons of cause and effect - that your thoughts, feelings, words and actions are causes set in motion – and that intention is a creative force, take into account the difference between empowering language and disempowering language.

When you are invited to a dinner party Friday night, and you say "I will try to be there", what you are implying is, "I will not be there, but do not have the courage to say so."

When you say "I should exercise more often", what you are implying is, "it would be wise for me to exercise more often, but I am not going to do so."

When you say, "Do not forget to turn the lights off before leaving the house," what you also said is "forget to turn the lights off before leaving the house."

When you say, "I am against war", you are thinking about war.

Alternatively, more empowering statements are:

"I would enjoy your dinner party Friday night, but cannot commit to being there."

"I know that regular exercise is good for me, but that is not a priority in my life right now, as evidenced by my actions."

"Remember to turn the lights off before you leave the house."

"I am in favor of peace."

Positive, affirming, decisive language, including your internal dialogue and communication with others, plants the seeds of intention and causality in a constructive manner. Disempowering language will lead to a life full of excuses, broken promises and half-achieved goals, rather than a life built on the solid foundation of keeping your word, achieving your objectives, and enjoying a feeling of confidence and fulfillment.

Intention is a creative force.

Your thoughts, feelings, WORDS and actions are causes set in motion.

Everything you do has consequences.

Thus, it is wise to be mindful of the words you use, and the intentions you set.

> You are always setting intentions,
> and setting causes into motion,
> with the words you speak.

How then do you speak to yourself? How do you speak to other people?

Are the words you use indicative of defeat, failure and lack of belief? Or are they positive, affirming, inspiring, uplifting and indicative of belief?

Do you speak to yourself and others with judgment, shaming, blaming and discouragement? Or with dignity, respect, kindness, validation and encouragement?

> Be mindful of your language,
> for it has creative power.

To say "You should try not to use the words should and try" is, of course, a fun play on words, but serious as well. Pay attention to what you say and how you say it. Remember to use empowering language.

OPPOSITE

Have you ever had a conversation with someone who insists that you only use language that is to their liking? They feel it is their duty to correct you whenever you use words that are not optimal – in their opinion. They will demand that you rephrase your statements using wording that they perceive as more enlightened. People like this genuinely believe that forcing their unsolicited advice upon you, and refusing to allow you to express yourself as you choose, is a service to you. In actuality, it is incredibly annoying. Such people are pretending to be highly conscious, but are in fact completely un-self-aware, and highly obnoxious.

It is perfectly fine to use whatever words you choose in order to express yourself. And please, for the sake of all humanity, do not be one of these people just described.

However, as a general rule of thumb, for your own sake, you should try not to use the words "should" and "try". Instead, be deliberate in your creative self-expression, by using empowering language

PART FIVE

Lessons And Learning

CHAPTER 22

Always Keep Learning

Learning is a lifelong process.

A well-known Bob Dylan lyric that cannot be directly quoted for legal reasons suggests that a person is either busy growing or decaying, becoming or dying.

You will never know everything. You can always learn more. Every day is an opportunity for learning and growth. In fact, you are always learning new things throughout your life, whether you are aware of it or not.

Learning can be informal, like collecting wisdom through your life experiences. It can be more intentional, like watching video tutorials and studying online courses. It can be more structured and formal, as in actual classroom education.

You can keep learning just for the fun of it. If you start learning how to play the banjo today, five years from now, you will be a far better banjo player than if you never begin at all. You might even enjoy yourself!

Muscles atrophy when not exercised. The same is true for your brain. Use it or lose it, they say. Exercise your mind regularly. Always keep learning.

What are you learning today?

What are your life experiences teaching you?

What more would you like to learn? Get on it!

OPPOSITE

There will be times in your life when you do not feel like continuously learning and growing. Give yourself a break. Go to the beach, or grill some tacos with your friends, and just relax.

However, as a general rule of thumb, there is no opposite to this life lesson that will serve you well. Remember that learning is a lifelong process. Always keep learning.

CHAPTER 23

Apply What You Learn

If you learn something, but do not apply what you have learned, did you really learn it?

Learning is useless unless you apply what you learn.

The purpose of learning something is to use your new information, whether it is for fun, for profit, or for the betterment of yourself and the world.

Some folks suspect that the reason for being alive in human form is to learn and to grow. If this is true, then you must learn, and apply what you have learned, in order to fulfill your purpose in this lifetime.

Playing a musical instrument is a great example. The only way to improve is through study and practice. You must apply what you learn.

What about your own life? Consider how much you have already learned and apply regularly.

Every time you apply what you have learned, you become more of a master of life.

Have you ever made mistakes in relationships? Have you learned anything useful about how to relate to, interact with, and treat other people? Do you think that, when confronted with similar situations in the future, you may be able to respond more wisely than you did in the past? Will you be able to apply what you have learned?

This is a good start. Now, go out there and apply what you have learned. Otherwise, you are just wasting your time, and everyone else's.

OPPOSITE

An apparent opposite to this life lesson could be that sometimes you just want to learn something because it will expand your worldview. Yet, even then, you are applying what you have learned, by having a broader vision and understanding of the way the world is. So, there appears to be no opposite to this life lesson.

Always keep learning. Then, apply what you learn.

CHAPTER 24

Life's Lessons Keep Getting Louder Until You Learn Them

Life offers you lessons. You can choose to learn them or not.

Sometimes, you encounter the same lesson repeatedly, until you have learned it. Often, the longer it takes for you to learn and apply a lesson, the louder and more painful that lesson becomes. Life's lessons keep getting louder until you learn them.

You can identify persistent lessons by noticing where you may continue to have the same challenges or roadblocks in your life. When a big problem arises, it could be that you did not heed the earlier warning signs, when they were first presented to you in more gentle forms.

Learning your lessons sooner rather than later will allow you to avoid previous pitfalls, end undesirable cycles that produce negative results, and live a life of greater grace and ease.

Learn your lessons while the consequences are still manageable, before they become too big, too loud and too disastrous.

Some folks believe that the purpose of human existence is to learn and to grow. Believe this or not, life is a classroom – you have no choice in this matter. You have learned a lot in your life up until now. You will continue to learn more until the day you die. Learning is inevitable. So learn your lessons. The sooner the better.

OPPOSITE

It is not necessarily always true that each and every life lesson continues to get louder and more painful until you learn it. However, enough people have discovered this phenomenon that it is worth including in this book and understanding in your life.

Furthermore, as master Jeffrey Boehme has suggested, learning and growth can come from joy, not just from suffering. For example, you may discover certain behaviors that enhance your lovemaking. By learning and applying these lessons, life will be better for you and your partner, all based off of joy, not suffering.

Thus, there may be opposites to this life lesson. Yet, by remembering that some life lessons become louder until you learn them, you can preclude difficulties from arising by heeding the lessons that arise in front of you, rather than ignoring them.

CHAPTER 25

Teach Through Your Way Of Being

No one likes to be criticized or invalidated. If someone is behaving inappropriately, they will most likely not respond well if you confront them directly on their inappropriate behavior.

A more constructive approach is to model wise behavior.

Rather than tell someone, "You need to listen to me when I talk to you", you can model for them what that looks like, by listening while they talk to you.

Rather than tell someone, "You need to exercise more," you can model for them what a lifestyle that includes exercise looks like.

Of course, some people are so dense and unaware that no matter how much you model wise behavior, they will never catch the clue.

However, in general, it is a good idea to model wise behavior rather than verbally instructing people how they must behave. If you simply demonstrate appropriate action, there is a chance that they will notice your teaching, either consciously or subconsciously.

"Lead by example" is a common phrase, which suggests the same idea. If you think it is a good idea for people to be kind to one another, then be kind. This is enough.

"Do as I say, not as I do" is another common phrase, which mocks those who do not abide by their own teachings. You can avoid such criticism by doing as you do, and then you will not have to say anything.

It is a common phenomenon for spiritual gurus to be discovered as scoundrels or frauds. They preach wholesome concepts, but do not live them. Their actions do not match their words.

In contrast, some of the greatest spiritual teachers have no titles, teach no classes, and wear no golden robes. They simply teach their lessons such as presence, kindness and integrity through their daily actions and regular ways of being.

Do you know great teachers who spread their message with their actions, rather than their words?

What about yourself? What are you teaching others through your behavior?

The next time you want to tell someone how they can behave more wisely, instead, choose to demonstrate what that behavior looks like.

OPPOSITE

Obviously, if you are teaching knowledge – a particular skill or subject – you will need to use words.

At other times, someone may be acting so inappropriately that you must speak up and tell them to knock it off.

Thus, there are exceptions to this life lesson.

However, as a general rule of thumb, when it comes to ways of behaving in this world, it is better to teach through your way of being, rather than telling people how to behave.

CHAPTER 26

Reject Other People's Limiting Beliefs

No belief is certain.

If you know something to be true or false, it is not a belief, it is a knowing.

A belief is an adherence to a concept, as if it were true, without knowing for certain.

Now, the power of the mind, as evidenced by the placebo effect, can turn a belief into a reality, even if at first it is not true. This is the power of belief. Imagine if someone holds a limiting belief that is not true. If you accept their limiting belief, you can make it true, thereby imposing false limits on yourself.

At other times, beliefs hold no power at all. If it is raining, and you believe you will not get wet, step outside and test the power of your belief.

Sometimes beliefs can alter reality, other times they have no impact whatsoever. Either way, this life lesson holds true: Reject other people's limiting beliefs.

Other people's limiting beliefs can only hold you back in life. If such beliefs have no influence on reality, then it is useless to consider them. If such beliefs can indeed alter reality, it will only reduce your world of possibilities. Therefore, always reject other people's limiting beliefs.

Reject Other People's Limiting Beliefs

Parents, peers and others are often ready to discourage your dreams. They think they are being helpful, encouraging you to "be realistic". Or they are simply treating you the way that others have treated them. They are generally unaware of their disparaging behavior. But you can become aware of it, and disallow it.

Have you ever noticed how some folks constantly put others down and discourage them? Have you noticed how these folks are not the ones accomplishing great things? They probably took on the limiting beliefs of others who influenced them. Then, rather than living fruitful, fulfilling and fantastic lives, they live mediocre, if not pathetic lives, passing along their negativity, defeatism and acceptance of failure.

These people confuse possibilities with certainty, beliefs with knowing. They seek to impose their feeble opinions upon you as if they were facts.

> **Never have those who accomplished great things allowed the voices of other people's doubts to discourage them from their achievements.**

Some folks are pessimistic. Tell them you are training to climb a mountain or run a marathon; they will tell you it is too difficult. Tell them you are starting a business; they will tell you that most businesses fail. Tell them you want to write a book; they will tell you that most authors only sell 200 copies of their published works. These are the types of limiting beliefs to reject. These are the types of people to ruthlessly eliminate from your life.

First, notice when people seek to discourage you. They think they know how the world works, and insist on offering you their unsolicited advice, as if they are being helpful.

Second, evaluate if they are mistaking their beliefs for truth, or if there is merit to their caution.

Third, reject their limiting beliefs, unless they are offering wise words of warning.

> You have every right to eliminate
> negative people from your life.
> Anyone who discourages you has got to go.

You can give them compassion from a distance. You can even pray for them. And here is some unsolicited advice for you right now my friend:

> Have a zero-tolerance policy in your life
> for people who seek to impose their
> limiting beliefs on you. Only allow people
> into your life who uplift and encourage you.

Next, take a look at yourself. Do you seek to impose your limiting beliefs on other people, discouraging them from living their greatest lives? Or do you uplift, support and encourages others? What kind of person would you prefer to be? What kind of people would you prefer to be around?

Perhaps you cannot eliminate all discouraging people from your life. It could be a parent or spouse who seeks to impose their limiting beliefs on you. Perhaps you need to look them squarely in the eyes, and tell them to knock it off.

Whether or not you can successfully remove all negative people from your life, you must stand firmly and unshakably grounded in your truth and recognize that other people's facts are usually just opinions.

Then, you can reject other people's limiting beliefs.

OPPOSITE

If you want to jump off a cliff, thinking you can fly unassisted by flying devices, and someone seeks to discourage you from doing so, it may be wise to listen. This is an obvious example.

A more nuanced example could be that you want to invest in a business, but your friend has personal knowledge of the others involved, and feels compelled to warn you about them based on their experience.

Situational awareness and discernment are required, when deciding whether or not to heed the advice of others. When are you being irrational, and another person is offering true wisdom? When is someone confusing their beliefs for facts, thereby seeking to hold you back unnecessarily? Usually you can figure out when to reject other people's limiting beliefs, and when to listen.

CHAPTER 27

Learn To Say I Don't Know

Confidence is sexy. Arrogance is not.

Some things you know with certainty. If you are an auto mechanic, you know how to fix a car. If you are a baker, you know how to bake a cake.

Most things you do not know with certainty. You have beliefs that cannot be proven. Learn to question your beliefs. Learn to distinguish between what you know for sure and what are possibilities to consider.

Have you ever tried to hold a conversation with someone who thought they knew everything? People like this are often unwilling to listen to you express yourself, unless what you say matches exactly what they believe. People like this will negate everything you say unless it fits their world view. This is pride, not confidence.

It is difficult to have an intelligent conversation with such people, and rather unpleasant to discuss concepts of any depth, meaning, subtlety, complexity or nuance. It can be like arguing with a hungry, tired five-year-old child about whose favorite dinosaur is superior.

In light of the possibility that few things can be known with absolute certainty, and that most people mistake their beliefs for facts, consider saying "I don't know" every time you hold a belief that you cannot prove.

How can you distinguish between a belief and a knowing? Every time you think you know something, ask yourself, "how do I know this to be true?" Without a clear and honest answer, it is a belief, not a knowing.

As soon as you think you know the truth, you become closed to all other possibilities and perspectives, and perhaps unpleasant to converse with. It is like the allegory of the cup full of water. You cannot pour more water into the cup because it is already full. If you already know everything, you cannot learn anything new.

> There are not many guarantees in life.
> However, one guarantee is that
> you do not know everything.

To say "I don't know" is more honest and constructive than claiming to know everything. It is also far less obnoxious.

When you say "I don't know", you become open to listening to other people's ideas and perspectives. You can consider numerous possibilities, without being attached to any one. You can have an adult conversation. You may even find that you can change your worldview when confronted with new information.

When you say "I don't know", it creates connection, rather than separation, between people on different sides of an issue. A dialogue is opened up. You can seek to understand other people, and find common ground. It may be easier to get along with others, because you are flexible and you are willing to listen, rather than invalidate them, thinking you know more than they do. It will certainly build trust.

This requires humility, because you may discover that you adhere rigidly to beliefs and opinions that cannot be proven, and may be incorrect. However, it is liberating to be able to change your mind, and let go of beliefs that are not true.

See if you can catch yourself today, acting like you know the truth but cannot verify it. Or catch yourself arguing with someone about the nature of reality. See if you can change your approach, and instead say "I don't know".

OPPOSITE

Sometimes, you do know. If you know, you know. It is okay to know something with certainty. Applied wisdom is knowing what you know, and what you do not.

Aside from those infrequent occasions when you are absolutely certain of an incontrovertible truth, it is usually a good idea to say "I don't know". Allow for and consider various possibilities, rather than insisting that your unprovable beliefs are facts. It is more authentic than pretending you know, when you do not.

CHAPTER 28

Never Trust An Expert

Be wary of anyone who thinks they know everything. At the very least, such people are foolish and annoying. At worst, they can be quite dangerous.

Confidence can be quite a turn on. It is reassuring when someone speaks with certainty. It works well in teaching, sales, dating, leadership, and really, in any human exchange.

However, pride and arrogance can be confused for confidence. Develop the ability to discern when someone is overly confident, rather than quietly self-assured.

To call oneself an expert may be accurate, or it may be an overstatement. To admit that there is always more to learn, and always the possibility to make mistakes, is great wisdom.

Certainly, there are experts in their fields, skilled masters of their crafts. Generally, they do not need to tell you that they are experts. Their work speaks for itself and it will be evident by what other people say about them.

The idea here is to be wary of self-proclaimed, self-promoting experts. If other folks call them experts, that has more credibility. The key here is to be cautious of outspoken pride versus quiet confidence.

A master is humble, not proud. Even a master makes mistakes, and has room to grow. Once someone calls themselves an expert, they may not be teachable, thinking they already know everything. A master only becomes a master by continually learning, and has made more mistakes than anyone else. They will display a calm confidence in their abilities, whereas a self-proclaimed expert may have more egoic pride attached to their abilities, rather than a humble knowing. A true expert will spend more time doing what they are good at than telling you about it.

OPPOSITE

Sometimes people truly are experts. It is wonderful to work with, train with and study with people at the top of their fields. Especially when others can attest to their expertise.

Furthermore, sometimes experts need to advertise themselves as such, in order to find customers or students, and their advertisements are truthful – they are indeed experts.

Yet, proceed with caution when someone calls themselves an expert. Be wary of anyone who thinks they know everything.

Definitely seek to hire, work with, train with, and learn from specialists, people who are knowledgeable, skilled and experienced. But be cautious when trusting an expert.

CHAPTER 29

A Master Often Wears Plain Clothes

It has been said that today's modern world is the Age of Prophets for Profit.

You are wise to be on guard against any self-proclaimed experts. So too are you wise to be cautious of those who label themselves Master, Guru, Shaman, Goddess, Priestess, Healer or other similar such titles.

There are countless folks promoting themselves as spiritual teachers, guides, healers, gurus, shamans and masters. They all fall somewhere along the spectrum of wisdom, skill, power, integrity and authenticity:

Some are wise and humble masters, who genuinely care to serve their students and followers, share their wisdom, and contribute to the betterment of humanity. Others are aspiring masters, still learning to lead and spread their message. Some are troubled souls who still have a long way to go on their own healing journeys. Others are alcoholics, womanizers or thieves. Some are first and foremost business people. Others believe they know and disseminate great truths, but are actually misguided and full of nonsense, or partial truths at best. Yet others are downright frauds.

This is not to denigrate all Prophets for Profit.

It is perfectly acceptable for people to make a living by teaching what they know, and selling products and services that benefit their customers. There are a great number of higher truths, healing modalities, spiritual practices and sparkling waters with merit and value that are being sold to modern seekers who can afford them.

The man dressed all in white with a long grey beard and the woman draped in golden robes with a feather in her hair may have great wisdom to offer you, albeit for a price. However, be wary of those who wear fancy clothing and use trendy cliché language, but may still be ruled by their own dark shadows of pride, lust, greed, arrogance, anger and other traits not generally ascribed to true masters.

The point here is to differentiate between a pretty package full of contrived spiritual propaganda versus true wisdom, depth, substance and meaning.

Learn to distinguish between a showman and a wise man.

How often are spiritual gurus discovered to be dishonest, unethical, hypocritical, abusive, self-serving scoundrels? In contrast, how often does an unknown man work an honest job, remain faithful to his wife and raise a good family? Which of these men is the true master?

Often, the true spiritual masters wear plain clothes and lead quiet lives.

They may cuss and smoke and drink. They may not go to church on Sundays or meditate at dawn or practice yoga at vegan retreats. They may not use the fashionable lingo of the day, wear the customary garb, or know the first thing about the Sanskrit language, Eastern philosophy, quartz crystals or sacred geometry. However, their way of being is their teaching. They do not need to announce to you how spiritually advanced they are. They are simply decent people living moral lives.

There is great value in being able to distinguish between authentic substance and superficial glamour. Often, inferior products are highly promoted. For example, some inexpensive processed foods and sweet carbonated beverages may come to mind. Society is constantly bombarded by suggestions that consuming such unhealthy products will make them feel better and be more likeable. Many folks succumb to these pervasive persuasions, as ridiculous as they are.

Meanwhile, superior products may be plain and uninteresting in comparison. Think of leafy green plants grown in your garden in contrast to food-like items sold at "super" markets and fast-food "restaurants".

The same is true with ideas and teachers. Often, poor ideas receive great publicity, while deeper truths and greater wisdom receive little attention, being plain and boring in comparison.

Be mindful that not all self-described masters are true masters. A real guru may not present himself as such. A real shaman will never tell you he is a shaman. A real goddess does not title herself so.

Thus, you are wise to exercise discernment when confronted with a master who has all the trappings of a guru and bears glorious titles.

Remember, a true master often wears plain clothes.

OPPOSITE

There are true masters in this world. Not all of them are undercover. Not all self-described masters are frauds. Often, a wise teacher must call themselves a master to promote themselves, find students, and offer their teachings to a wide audience. Some will share with you information and practices that will be life-enhancing, perhaps even life-changing, while remaining more or less humble and authentic.

Yet, be cautious of glamorous Prophets for Profit. Be wary of trendy gurus with grandiose titles, pretentious wardrobes and cliché vocabularies. Pay close attention to what they say, what they teach, how they behave, and their subtle energies too. By exercising keen observation and discernment, you can navigate away from the false prophets, and towards the true masters.

However, this can be tricky. Millions of people have succumbed to sales pitches from smooth showmen who pose as spiritual leaders. Good luck out there, and remember: A master often wears plain clothes.

CHAPTER 30

Never Trust A Thin Chef Or A Fat Personal Trainer

It will serve you well to learn to discern between people who act like they know what they are talking about, and people who really do know what they are talking about.

Do you want to study business from a professor who has never left the halls of academia, or from a successful entrepreneur? Do you want to study art with an accomplished artist, or a child with crayons? Do you want to learn how to build a house from a bookkeeper or a carpenter?

> Look for signs that someone can successfully implement their knowledge, not just talk about it.

For instance, chefs are generally plump, because they love food, including their own cuisine. A trustworthy chef loves to eat her creations. Her stout stature is a testament to her skill and passion as a chef. Would you trust a chef who does not eat what she cooks?

Likewise, a skilled and knowledgeable personal trainer is generally fit. If he knows how to get in shape and stay in shape, one can reasonably expect him to demonstrate this through his own behaviors. The results will be self-evident. Would you trust an unfit personal trainer who does not exercise?

> A fat chef likes to eat her own food,
> so she is probably a good chef.
> A fit personal trainer knows how to
> get in shape and stay in shape.

Be wary of self-proclaimed experts. Be cautious of glamorous gurus. Be suspicious of people who like to talk about what they can do. Seek to identify people who put their knowledge into action and teach through their way of being. Seek to identify people who do not tell you what they can do, but show you. Notice when people's actions match their words, and when their lifestyles reflect their expertise.

Never trust a thin chef, or a fat personal trainer.

OPPOSITE

Obviously, there are exceptions to this life lesson.

A skilled personal trainer may suffer an injury and become immobile and out of shape.

A chef familiar with the benefits of intermittent fasting and the inverse relationship of longevity to food consumption may be lean, not plump. Yet, the underlying premise remains the same: Trust people who are knowledgeable not only in word, but in action.

In such hypothetical situations, as with many life lessons presented in this book, situational awareness and discernment will help you identify nuances and exceptions.

As a general rule of thumb, pay heed to those who demonstrate a congruency between their words and their actions, and whose behaviors illustrate the practical application of their wisdom and knowledge.

PART SIX

A Few General Lessons

CHAPTER 31

If It Ain't A Hell Yes, It's A Hell No

This life lesson can be applied situationally.

Some folks will eat any food that is available to them, because they are hungry. Others are more selective, eating only the food that is a Hell Yes for them.

Some folks will take any job they can get, because they need to earn a living. Others are fortunate enough to only take work that is a Hell Yes for them.

Some folks will date and have sex with just about any willing participant. Others, even if they love intimacy, romance and sex, are more selective about their partnerships, only dating and sleeping with another that is a Hell Yes for them.

The basic principle is to be selective in your life. Honor your preferences and desires. Stick to your guns. Be careful where you focus your attention and spend your energy. Be selective in your endeavors.

Every day, you make numerous choices. Make the best choices you can. Listen to yourself, and make choices that excite you.

Most folks are not content with mediocrity. If they order a mediocre dish at a restaurant, they will not be satisfied. If they work at a mediocre job, they will be looking for a new one. If they go on a mediocre date, they will not pursue a relationship.

Regrets in life are often the result of poor decisions or accepting mediocrity. Most folks regret choosing a menu item, a job or a partner that they do not strongly prefer. These are a few examples, yet this principle can be applied to any area of your life. It is often optional, sometimes imperative.

If you are going to marry someone, make sure you are a Hell Yes for that person, and that they are a Hell Yes for you. If you are going to have children, you absolutely better be a Hell Yes for that too.

It may be impractical to apply this lesson to every area of your life at all times. However, at least some of the time, and especially for things that truly matter, it will serve you well to remember, if it ain't a Hell Yes, it's a Hell No.

OPPOSITE

Time does not stop marching forward. You need to continue living, even when conditions are not optimal. It may be unreasonable to only proceed down the most preferable pathways at all times. You may need to work a paying job, eat a nourishing meal, or spend time in the arms of a welcoming lover, even when the circumstances are not ideal.

Next, go one step further, to the true opposite. Turn this lesson upside down: Some folks enjoy saying yes to everything, looking forward to the opportunities, adventures and surprises that await them. They do not wait for perfect conditions to arise before engaging in life. They say, if it ain't a Hell No, make it a Hell Yes. They are curious to know, what does life have to offer me today?

Do what you need to survive in this turbulent world. Be open to the unknown and expand your horizons. However, from time to time, take a stand for what you truly prefer.

CHAPTER 32

When You Stop Searching, It Shows Up

Sometimes, the more you want something, the more difficult it is to obtain. When you stop caring or searching, it shows up effortlessly and unexpectedly.

When you strive too hard after an unrealized objective, you are resisting the world being the way it is, and the world may push back against you.

When you stop focusing on your desire, and go more gracefully with the natural flow of life, you create space for your desire to arise organically.

This is a challenging lesson to apply, because the stronger your desire for a particular outcome, the harder it can be to let it go.

> Often, the best things come to you
> when you least expect them, when
> you are least looking for them.

Have you ever experienced this phenomenon? Have you ever gotten a job or a date when you were not seeking them? Have you ever desired a new job or partner, and found yourself striving unsuccessfully towards these ends? Have you ever found what you were looking for as soon as you stopped looking?

Currently, what are your strongest unfulfilled desires? Are you struggling to attain them? Can you let them go?

Gently set your intentions for what you desire, but hold these desires loosely. Gracefully surrender to the flow of life. Allow the world to be exactly as it is, and shift your focus elsewhere.

Focus on yourself, do your inner work, do your outer work, take care of what you need to do. When you encounter other people, give your focus to them. Be present and listen. Give them the gift of your time and attention.

Be present to your moment-by-moment experiences. Be ready to respond skillfully to all situations that may arise. Be prepared to take advantage of the opportunities that present themselves. Expect the unexpected. You never know when you could be surprised.

Easier said than done, yet something you can work on today.

OPPOSITE

This lesson has its opposite. Energy follows thought, thought becomes matter, what you focus on grows, and with deliberate intention you can often create your desired results.

Great accomplishments are achieved with persistent focus and effort. You may find a job by sending out 100 resumes, or find a partner by going on 100 dates. If you wish to make one million dollars, you are more likely to do so with dedication and commitment. Sometimes, tenacity and perseverance are required for you to fulfill your dreams.

Yet, be mindful of the times in your life when the more you desire something, the more you may be pushing it away. Be mindful of when it is wise to focus on your desires, and when it is wise to let them go, and go with the flow.

Remember that life can be unexpected, and often, when you stop looking for something, it shows up.

CHAPTER 33

Happiness Is Not An Inside Job

One of the most popular, and most damaging pieces of misleading information in modern psychology being perpetuated by new age prophets for profit is the idea that "Happiness is an inside job".

For an enlightened master, yes, it is. For everyone else, no, it is not. If you wish to become an enlightened master, then go for it. You must find happiness solely and exclusively from within yourself.

However, this concept sets up a nearly impossible objective for the vast majority of people to strive after. You will probably fall short of this ideal, forever feeling like there is something wrong with you, endlessly chasing your tail in circles, and perpetually feeling inferior to the gurus who claim to be happy no matter what.

The idea that "happiness is an inside job" is based on the idea that you are completely responsible for everything in your reality. However, the truth is that, although you have some impact over your external world, you are also impacted by it. To an extent, you can "manifest" the life and reality you desire. To another extent, outside influences, such as the circumstances of your life and your surrounding environment, are always impacting you.

Forces outside of yourself probably influence your level of happiness. Anyone who tells you otherwise is not being intellectually honest.

Now, with personal agency, you can take actions to change your life's circumstances and your surroundings. You can also choose how you respond to the world.

Thus, rather than blaming external influences for your internal state of being, you can be proactive about creating an environment more conducive to happiness, and take responsibility for how you respond to life.

Yet, it remains that, while you have an effect upon your outside world, your outside world also has an effect upon you. If you have food and shelter, your bills are paid, you have good health and meaningful pursuits, if you have good company and loving relationships, you have fertile grounds for happiness to arise and thrive.

Conversely, if you are cold, wet, sick, hungry, homeless, broke and alone, your base layer of existence is like nutrient-deficient soil in which you hope to grow food. It is not an ideal environment for cultivating life to its fullest potential. You may find it more difficult to be happy under such circumstances.

> If you are cold, wet, sick, hungry, penniless and alone, it is more difficult to be happy than if you are safe, warm, dry, well-fed and well-loved.

If you do not believe this, you can listen to what the research has to say:

A study by Princeton University discovered that happiness increases with increased income, up until the point one has sufficient resources to live comfortably. These results indicate that having one's basic survival needs met facilitates happiness. That is, external forces such as having food, clothing, shelter and security can positively impact your inner state of being. It is easy to imagine that lacking these basic needs can cause fear, anxiety, worry, stress and unhappiness.

Perhaps you have experienced this yourself?

Harvard University did a 75-year study on what makes people happy, and discovered that the number one indicator of a person's happiness was the quality of their loving relationships. That is correct. It is the relationships with people whom you love, and who love you, or the lack of such people in your life, that will cause you to be happier, or less happy. More so than money, career success, fame, your contributions to society or how much yoga and meditation you do, your loving relationships will impact your happiness. Here again, it is something outside of one's self that, for most people, has a substantial influence on their happiness.

The leading indicator of your happiness is the loving relationships in your life.

This is corroborated by Johann Hari's TED talk: "Everything you think you know about addiction is wrong." He states that "The opposite of addiction is not sobriety. The opposite of addiction is connection." Check it out.

There are a few key takeaways in this book. One is the value of connection with other people. Your close, loving human relationships are of primary importance. This cannot be overstated. You must make this a top priority in your life, or you will forever remain unfulfilled.

Your external environment can and does exert an influence on your internal state of being. Therefore, do not make yourself crazy by wondering why you cannot simply choose to be happy. You will be wise to acknowledge that having your basic survival needs met, including food, shelter, a basic level of security, and loving relationships, does not guarantee your happiness, but can facilitate it.

Of course, be on guard against relying solely on external factors for your happiness. Perpetually seeking pleasure and fulfillment outside of yourself will never fill your inner void. You must do your inner work. Find peace within yourself, regardless of external circumstances, as best as you can.

Furthermore, if you are unhappy, it serves no constructive purpose to blame your life's circumstances or your surroundings.

You have it within you to change your environment, and create external conditions more conducive to happiness than your present ones.

The environment you create for yourself is important. When your basic needs are met, you are more likely to be happy. If not, it is up to you to create conditions in your life to satisfy them. In this sense, happiness IS an inside job, because it is dependent upon you to cultivate an outer environment conducive to inner peace and happiness.

However, cut yourself some slack. Understand that certain external factors influence your inner state of being. Happiness is not (entirely) an inside job.

OPPOSITE

Okay, this life lesson is both true and false at the same time. Happiness really is an inside job, and everyone knows it.

It is theoretically possible for you to achieve inner peace and happiness completely from within, your life circumstances and outer environment notwithstanding.

Consider the stories of the yogis in India, who sit with turbans on their heads and loin cloths around their waists. With long shaggy beards they meditate. With hands outstretched cradling empty bowls, they beg for food. Reports of these men suggest that they are in perpetual states of bliss. They have found happiness from within, even when they are cold, wet, sick, hungry and alone.

You too can achieve this state of being, if you so desire. Go for it! Get rid of everything you own, strap a diaper around your waist, and go sit on the street meditating.

> Eat only the food you receive from begging, and perhaps you can prove that happiness is entirely an inside job.

However, the reality is that if you are cold, wet, sick, hungry, broke and alone, you have less fertile ground upon which to be happy than if you are warm, dry, healthy, well-fed and well-loved.

Of course, having all the creature comforts in life does not guarantee happiness. Continuously seeking to fill your inner void through the endless pursuit of sensory stimulation and short-term satisfaction will achieve a temporary distraction from the pain of existence and the presence of being, but will never deliver true happiness and inner peace.

You are wise to practice meditation, to connect with the source consciousness and love that you are, or somehow find a way to derive happiness internally, independent of external forces.

There is a balance between finding peace and happiness from within, and understanding that, unless you are an enlightened master, outside influences will facilitate or hinder your ability to do so. Therefore, you may wish to consider the benefits of seeking to meet your basic survival needs, and enjoy loving relationships in your life.

Remember that, for most human beings, happiness is not (entirely) an inside job.

CHAPTER 34

Problem = Challenge = Opportunity

Part of being human is experiencing difficulties in life.

This is the first of Buddha's principal teachings. "Life is suffering". A more nuanced understanding of this teaching is that life contains unsatisfactory conditions and experiences, ranging from mild discomfort to excruciating pain.

Everyone has a unique disposition and temperament. Some folks can gracefully and easily handle anything that life throws their way, while others find great difficulty with even the slightest disturbance.

This is where you have control over your life, by choosing wisely the words you use, and how you frame a situation. Everyone has problems. Sometimes they are insurmountable. Usually, they are solvable.

Can you recall a time in your life when you faced an overwhelming challenge? Yet, after doing the work to overcome it, you look back and it appears as only a small and temporary inconvenience?

This happens throughout your life. There was a time when learning to count from one to ten was a big deal. Now, it is second nature. Do you remember the first time you mounted a bicycle, how difficult and possibly scary it was? How many difficulties in your life looked mighty in the future, yet miniscule in retrospect?

Reframing how you see the difficulties in your life can assist you in overcoming obstacles and even leveraging your hardships for growth.

Think about a problem in your life.
Now, rethink of it as a challenge.
Then, discover what the opportunity is.

If you first convert every problem in your life into a challenge, then to an opportunity, you will become a superhero, as you confront difficulties, solve problems, overcome obstacles, and seize every opportunity for resilience, expansion and creativity.

Easier said than done.

Start simply. Choose one thing. What is a problem in your life? It can be a small one, or it can be the biggest problem that you face.

Next: How can you rethink of this problem as a challenge to conquer?

Finally, what is the opportunity in facing and overcoming the challenge, thereby solving the problem? How will you feel, having resolved the situation? How will you benefit? How will your life have improved?

Come on now, you superhero. Take advantage of the opportunity to overcome your challenges and solve your problems.

OPPOSITE

Sometimes, situations arise that are simply problematic. Converting them first to a challenge, then an opportunity may not be the wisest approach. Just deal with the problem.

With situational awareness and discernment, you will know when you can benefit from applying this life lesson.

PART SEVEN

How To Live

CHAPTER 35

Be More Loving

Yes. That is all.

Be more loving.

Do everything with love.

Stop judging other people. Allow everyone to be that which they are. Accept everyone as they are.

Give love. Be love. Be more loving. This is it.

If you do this, and this alone, you are well on your way to becoming an enlightened master.

Some of the greatest human needs are to be seen and heard, to be acknowledged and understood. To be accepted. To be valued. To be validated. To feel safe – physically and emotionally.

To be loved.

People want to be loved. People need to be loved. So do you. The lack of love is a root cause of countless problems in the world. Receiving love is one of the greatest medicines. Giving love is one of the greatest gifts. It costs you nothing, and causes everyone involved to feel good.

Considering the possibility that what you put out comes back to you, to give love is the wisest way of being.

Give the gift you most wish to receive. Give love. Be loving. No matter what. All the time. Wherever you go. To everyone.

Put this on for today. Go out into the world and be more loving.

OPPOSITE

On the surface of this life lesson there is no opposite. Always be loving.

However, sometimes there is evil in this world. It may not be wise to accept everyone as they are, at all times. When people are truly cruel or evil, do not accept their poor behavior.

On a more nuanced level, someone may behave in an unkind manner towards you. In this case, you certainly have the right to disallow them from your life. You can still practice compassion for this person, albeit from a safe distance.

Yet, if you have ever experienced anything that brings you into the truth of who you are, be it through entheogens, a spiritual practice, a near-death experience, a simple innate knowing, or by other means, you know that love is the answer.

Therefore, aside from egregious situations, as a general rule of thumb, there is no opposite to this life lesson that will serve you well.

Be more loving.

CHAPTER 36

Chop Wood, Carry Water

According to the internet, Chop Wood, Carry Water is an ancient proverb, whose true meaning is open to interpretation.

Back before modern luxuries made people soft, each person, family or community needed to be self-sufficient, taking care of all their own survival needs. Two of the most basic needs were wood and water.

Water is life. To grow food, keep animals, bathe, cook, clean and hydrate yourself – you must have water. Throughout time, people have had to carry water, from its source to where they used it, in order to sustain life.

Wood has traditionally been necessary for human life as well. Throughout history, wood has been used for shelter, warmth, light and cooking. People have had to chop wood for their survival. Before families and friends gathered around the television, they gathered around the campfire, since time immemorial.

To chop wood and carry water means to attend to your basic survival needs by performing the daily acts that sustain you. It means to take care of yourself, your responsibilities and the basic requirements of life. To elaborate, it means to earn a living, pay your bills, clean up after yourself, eat healthy and exercise, and be present with the ones you love.

There is a deeper implied meaning, which is to be present with the activity in which you are engaged. Immerse yourself in the experience. Be deliberate in the endeavor. Pay full attention to what you are doing, and do it well. When you are chopping wood, chop wood. Select the appropriate types of trees. Chop wood in the sizes and quantities you need. Do not cut your foot off. When you are carrying water, carry water. Select a clean source of water. Carry only the water you need. Do not spill it along your path.

In this modern world, life can be overly complex. To chop wood and carry water is to simplify. Take care of the basics, and do so with care.

Chop wood, carry water. Does it mean something more to you?

OPPOSITE

Another ancient concept is to take a day of rest, when there is no wood to chop nor water to carry. This is a wonderful idea. Take a weekly day of rest. However, to prepare for this day, you must chop extra wood and carry extra water the day before.

Thus, there is no opposite to this life lesson that will serve you well.

Take care of life's basic needs. Do so mindfully, with deliberate intention and care.

Chop wood, carry water.

CHAPTER 37

Ten Before Ten

This is a practical life lesson to be applied through taking persistent action. Sometimes, it is best not to force things. Other times, you must take action.

Be proactive with what is important to you. Create the life you want for yourself as best as you can. Take constructive action towards your desired outcomes. Do things that you enjoy, and that make you feel good.

Do ten things before ten in the morning. It could be to make ten sales calls, run ten kilometers, journal for ten minutes, read ten pages in a book, practice the banjo for ten minutes, or spend ten minutes of stillness and breathing when you first arise.

When you begin your day early, and get started on the right foot, you feel good about yourself, you set the tone for a productive day, and your life tends to move in a direction you desire and prefer.

Ten before ten originated as a salesman's mantra. When he made ten sales calls before ten in the morning, he added to his list of prospective clients who were genuinely interested in his products and services. He felt good about himself, and he had the rest of the day to prepare proposals and contracts, go to the gym or the beach, and spend time with his loved ones. When he did not accomplish his ten before ten, he felt stressed out, spent the rest of the day struggling to find new prospective clients, and failed to exercise, enjoy nature or attend to his family.

Whether or not you are a salesperson, when you apply the ten before ten life lesson, the way you conduct and experience your life will be noticeably upgraded, perhaps even extraordinary.

Sometimes, it serves you well to be still and do nothing. Other times, you must take action. One of the best ways of taking action is to commit to and fulfill the practice of ten before ten.

How can you apply this lesson in your life?

What is your ten before ten?

OPPOSITE

There is absolutely no opposite to this life lesson that will ever serve you well. Make a habit out of doing ten before ten, your life will only get better.

CHAPTER 38

Have A Practice

This life lesson cannot be overstated.

It sounds simple. It is simple. Yet it is also difficult, for it requires great discipline.

To have a practice is one of the most important things you can possibly do for yourself.

What is a practice?

Karate is a practice. Playing the banjo is a practice.

Meditation, yoga, chi gong, martial arts, playing music, singing and dancing are practices, if done regularly. Swimming, running, playing tennis, weightlifting, gardening and journaling can be practices. Sex can be a practice, if you approach it with consciousness.

A practice is something that you engage in regularly, with deliberate intention. It tends to be meditative and focused, and serves to bring you into present moment awareness. A practice generally requires self-discipline, and will often contain elements of self-cultivation and/or creative expression. You may find that you lose your sense of time and sense of self, while engaged in your practice. It may also cause you to feel amazing.

Having a practice is an anchor in your life. You return to it again and again. You do it consistently and build upon it. If your practice is yoga, you will become more flexible, and perhaps more calm and present. If your practice is karate, you will eventually earn a black belt, and so on. Ask anyone who already has a practice if it makes their life better or worse. You already know the answer to this question.

> The best practices are ones that cultivate, strengthen and refine your body, mind and spirit.

Do you already have one or more practices? Do you practice them regularly? Are you cultivating, strengthening and refining your mind, body and spirit?

If not, what can you choose as a practice? Will you practice it?

Have the self-discipline, desire, motivation and determination to have a practice, and practice consistently. It will enrich your life and your being. Eventually you may even master it.

OPPOSITE

There is absolutely no opposite to this life lesson that will ever serve you well.

If you do not already have a practice, find one. It is imperative that you have a practice.

CHAPTER 39

Practice, Practice, Practice

It does you no good to have a practice, if you do not practice.

First, choose a practice. Then, practice, practice, practice.

If you want to become a talented banjo player, there is only one way to do it. Can you guess what that is? If you want to earn a black belt in karate, there is only one way to achieve it. You already know what it is.

When you apply yourself consistently to one thing, you will become skilled, and perhaps even achieve mastery. You may wish to master something in your life. Although it will take commitment, dedication and self-discipline, you will probably enjoy it, too.

You absolutely must become skilled at something, if not a few things. The best way to become skilled at anything is to practice, practice, practice.

To practice is a habit. Form this habit for yourself. Practice regularly. Practice often. Practice every day, if you can.

Have you ever really enjoyed watching a live musical performance? Have you ever watched a masterful musician play their instrument? Have you ever thought to yourself, "Wow that musician is amazing!"? Have you ever considered how much time they have spent practicing? Some folks have natural talent. Some get started at a young age. Nonetheless, every time you hear a talented musician play, there is always one common element present in their music:

All skilled musicians have one shared ingredient: They have practiced, practiced and practiced.

Your age and natural talent are not the most important factors, if you wish to become a skilled banjo player. What matters is picking up a banjo, studying how to play it, and practicing consistently. Five years from now, either you will or will not be a talented banjo player.

There is only one factor that will make all the difference: practice, practice, practice.

On your first day of karate class, you might get your butt kicked. At the very least, you may feel incapable of defending yourself or kicking someone else's butt. If you go to class three days a week, have a quality instructor, and apply yourself diligently, you will eventually earn a black belt.

You get the point.

Do you already have a practice? If so, how is that going for you? Do you practice regularly? Are you highly skilled? Are you a master?

If you do not yet have a practice, consider what you will take on. What will you do every day? What will you enjoy being skilled at?

Once you have a practice, it is highly advisable – if not imperative – to practice, practice, practice.

OPPOSITE

There is absolutely no opposite to this life lesson that will ever serve you well. Do not settle for a mediocre existence. Achieve excellence at something. Have a practice, then practice, practice, practice.

CHAPTER 40

How You Practice Is How You Play

It has been said that "practice makes perfect". This is not true. Only perfect practice makes perfect.

To become a talented banjo player, you need to learn to play the right notes. If you are sloppy when you practice, often hitting wrong notes, do you think it will be any different when you are on stage performing?

John is a guitar player. He insists on never playing a wrong note when he practices. With every new song or exercise, he starts playing slowly, with mental clarity, attention and focus. He plays as slowly as he needs to in order to play each note correctly, the first time, and every time he plays. He only speeds up his playing when he has built the muscle memory to hit every note correctly, and knows he can do so. This requires great patience and self-discipline. Yet, John understands that only perfect practice makes perfect. His mind and body, working together, create a neural network of only playing correct notes. John is now a master guitarist. Every note he plays, every song he plays, is crisp, clear, note perfect and as fast or slow as he wishes it to be. How John practices is how he plays.

It is not enough to practice, practice, practice. You must practice correctly. Be deliberate and intentional in your practice. Pay attention to your technique. Go slow. Do it right. Practice with accuracy and precision. Eventually it will become second nature, almost effortless.

If you practice poorly, you are creating the muscle memory and neural networks to perform poorly.

This life lesson is evident with male sexuality. Boys often discover how to masturbate before they begin having sex with a partner. Generally, the focus is on the endpoint, rather than on the process itself.

Thus, boys develop the habit of ejaculating after a short period of self-pleasuring. Later in life, when men engage in intercourse, it is a common phenomenon for them to ejaculate before fully satisfying their partner. These men have trained themselves to complete the process quickly, rather than prolong the duration of their sexual stimulation. How they have practiced is how they play.

Now imagine if boys were to practice differently, how they might play differently as men. If a man wants to train himself to last long enough to fully satisfy his partner, he would be wise to practice stimulating himself for as long as possible before culminating the experience.

You can apply this lesson to every area of your life. Playing the banjo, practicing karate, having sex or anything else.

Be deliberate in your practices, because when it comes time to perform, you will play how you have practiced.

OPPOSITE

Every once in a while, an inexperienced person will have a stroke of luck. Conversely, someone who practices diligently may experience a failure.

However, as a general rule of thumb, there is absolutely no opposite to this life lesson that will ever serve you well.

Have a practice. Practice, practice, practice. Be mindful of how you practice, for how you practice is how you play.

CHAPTER 41

Your Life Is Your Practice

How you live your days is how you live your life. Your habits make you who you are.

Everything in your life is practice, whether you know it or not. You are always practicing.

With deliberate intention, you can make full use of this practice time.

Practice is not just when you are playing music, training martial arts, or if you are a man, learning to extend your sexual performance. Those are great places to start.

It continues when you are walking down the street, at work, interacting with other people or all by yourself.

Every moment is your practice. The ultimate practice is paying attention, and directing your mind's intention.

When you are alone, practice paying attention to yourself. Be intentional in your breathing. Notice how you are feeling, and what you are thinking. Notice your surroundings: the feeling of air rushing through your nose, the sun on your skin, the beauty of nature, the movement of life around you. It is a practice to consciously direct your mind's intention, to notice your inner and outer environments, rather than allowing your thoughts to arise randomly.

When you are with other people, practice being aware of how you interact with them. Do you smile or scowl? Do you listen attentively? Do you listen to understand, or to respond? Do you see and hear them? Do you notice their body language? Do you sense their subtle energies? Do you scan the room looking for someone more interesting or attractive to talk to? Even worse, do you denigrate, discourage or invalidate them? Are you wanting something from them? Or are you simply enjoying the interaction, curious to know who they are and what they have to express? Are you judging them or accepting them? Are you afraid that they may be judging you?

Practice noticing how you relate to other people.

> Every time you interact with another person, you are practicing the art of human relations.

When you are at work, is your mind on vacation, or are you focused attentively on the task at hand? Are you practicing doing your job well, or poorly?

Your entire life is your practice. This book is a collection of prompts to encourage you to practice with deliberate intention.

> Everything is training. All your past experiences have prepared you for today. How you train today will prepare you for tomorrow.

How you train every day prepares you for the rest of your life. The more attuned you are to your training, the more well prepared you are to meet what lies ahead.

Everything is training. Your life is your practice.

Everything you do, you can do mindfully or carelessly.

Everything you do in life is an opportunity to cultivate aptitude and skillfulness. Take advantage of the opportunities you encounter all day every day to practice.

How you live your days is how you live your life.

Your life is your practice.

How will you practice today?

OPPOSITE

There is absolutely no opposite to this life lesson that will ever serve you well.

Have a practice.

Practice, practice, practice.

How you practice is how you play.

Your life is you practice.

CHAPTER 42

Nothing Matters

On a geological time frame, absolutely nothing matters. One human life, compared to the time it takes for a glacier to carve a mountain, or a river to carve a canyon, is but the blink of an eye, in cosmic terms. From this perspective, one human life is statistically insignificant. It is negligible and therefore meaningless.

Phew, what a relief, right? Take a load off!

Whenever you are sad, angry or frustrated, when people and the world are not the way you want them to be, when things in life are not going your way, you can always remember: Nothing matters.

OPPOSITE

On a shorter timeframe, such as from your birth to your death, everything matters. Everything has impact. What you eat. The quality of your sleep. How you breathe. Your human and animal relationships. How you spend your time. Where you focus your attention.

Every thought, feeling, word and action is a cause set in motion. All causes have effects, all effects have causes. Your behaviors will have consequences, the effects of which may be inescapable.

This is especially true if reincarnation and karma are a real thing. You may have infinite lifetimes, and everything you do matters, regardless of the timeframe. It all adds up over time. Whether it is contained to a single lifetime, or extends through all of eternity, no one really knows.

> You may wish to consider that every act leaves
> an indelible mark on your permanent record.
> How then would you choose to behave?

Since you have been incarnated into human form, you get to choose to give meaning and energy to whatever you want.

Start by considering what you give energy to that does not serve you. See if you can ever so gently let those things go.

Then, consider what is truly important, and direct your focus, attention and energy in those directions.

> What is truly important to you? Ask
> yourself this question repeatedly. Continue
> answering until you run out of responses.

Give yourself some time. Think about it in the shower, or while you exercise. Allow your subconscious mind to work on this question while you sleep.

You might immediately know what is most important to you. Or, it could be that the more you answer this question, the more profound and revealing your answers will become.

Everyone is unique, their answers will vary. There are also some commonly important aspects of human existence. These may include:

Taking care of yourself.

Your health.

Satisfying your basic needs for survival and comfort: Safety, shelter, water, food, dryness and warmth.

Genuine human connection and loving relationships.

Physical touch and sex.

How you treat other people.

Laughter, and having fun.

The experiences of life: Seeing and doing things you enjoy, and that stimulate you.

Are these shared human priorities important to you?

Consider the commonalities you share with most people, and that the above items may be important to you.

Then, determine what is uniquely important to you. Get very clear on the answers to this question.

> Discover what is important to you.
>
> Discover what you most love about life.
>
> Make these things top priority.
>
> Let go of everything else, as best you can.
>
> Your time is running out.

CHAPTER 43

God Rewards Action

At times, swift, decisive action is necessary. If there is something you want to do, or need to do, do it now. The sooner the better.

Sitting around waiting for the phone to ring is not going to produce the same results as getting off your butt and making outbound phone calls. If you want to make money, get a date, create art, learn something new, stop your house from burning down when it catches fire, grow a vegetable garden, or accomplish anything in life, you must take action.

Obviously, humans are often taking action to sustain life. However, this life lesson is directed towards those areas of your life where you want to thrive.

You must be crystal clear about what is important to you. Then focus your attention, intention and energy, and take action.

Perhaps, what you desire will magically arrive in front of you, through no effort of your own other than simply thinking about it. However, you are more likely to achieve your desired objectives if you take action.

God, the Universe, or whichever your preferred fount of creation, responds to your intention and your behavior. As stated by the United States Internal Revenue Service in their 2022 Instructions for Form 2555:

> "Evidence of your intention may be your words and acts. If these conflict, your acts carry more weight than your words."

GOD REWARDS ACTION

God rewards action. Take massive action. Do not delay.

You may find that when you take action, the harder you work, the luckier you become. Take deliberate, intentional steps every day in the direction of your needs and your desires. Make no excuses. Take care of business, and create your preferred life and self as best as you can.

> The harder you work, the luckier you become.

Here is a practical exercise to get you started: Ask yourself, what is the one thing you would most love to have in your life, that you reasonably believe you can achieve? Then ask yourself, what actions can you take to bring this about?

Then, go do it. Get going today. Take committed, persistent action, and witness how God responds.

OPPOSITE

Sometimes, do nothing. Especially if you do not feel in alignment with what you are doing, or striving after. Then, taking action may be in vain. Sometimes, the more you struggle towards a goal, the more you are pushing it away.

Situational awareness and discernment can tell you when to do nothing, or when to take action and what actions to take.

Although there are times to be still, and times to avoid taking actions that are not in alignment, as a general rule of thumb, this life lesson will serve you well. God rewards action.

> You must take massive action towards fulfilling your life before you die. Or not. When you do, God rewards action.

CHAPTER 44

Do Not Delay

This is a corollary to the life lesson God Rewards Action. Do not take action tomorrow. Take action today.

> The best time to plant a tree was twenty years ago. The next best time to plant a tree is today.

When something needs to be done, do it immediately, or as soon as you possibly can.

When it is time to take action, do not delay.

Here is an example you can probably relate to:

Have you ever eaten a meal and not immediately washed your dishes afterwards? Are you familiar with the nuisance and struggle of cleaning the dried food remnants from those dishes at a later time, versus the relative ease of washing the dishes when the food residues are still fresh and moist?

Now, apply this analogy to every area of your life. Your entire existence will henceforth be far more fluid and less problematic, when you do not delay. You are welcome.

When you attend immediately to matters that must be addressed, life is easier. You resolve problems before they grow larger. You free up your attention so you can get on with your life, rather than be burdened with the psychic drag of unfinished business.

When you require medical attention, visit a doctor. Do not delay.

As soon as you discover male plants in your marijuana garden, eradicate them immediately. Do not delay.

When your needs are not being met by your partner in a relationship, speak up about it. Do not delay.

If you have a problem with another person, address it, do not delay. When you do not confront the issue, it can fester, and cause problems down the road. If you simply need to avoid them because they are toxic, or an energy vampire, get away from them as soon as possible, do not delay.

When it comes to problems in your life, they may grow larger when ignored. When you address them upfront, they often go away.

> If something troubles you, it will continue to trouble you, until you face it, head on.

With every problem or challenge in your life, address it directly, head on, as soon as possible. Do not delay.

If there is something constructive you wish to do in your life, the same rule applies. Get on with it, do not delay.

If you wish to become a skilled banjo player, the sooner you begin to study and practice the banjo, the sooner you will become a skilled banjo player. Do not delay.

> The best time to start saving for retirement was the day you began earning money. The next best time is today.

If you have a goal, go for it. Now. Know who you are, be clear about what is important to you, choose one thing, exercise self-discipline, focus, take immediate, decisive, and persistent action. Do not delay.

Whether it is a problem in your life, a goal you have, or simply washing the dishes while the food residues are still fresh on the plates, your life will be easier, more enjoyable and more fulfilling if you take action today.

Be aware of your challenges and be clear in you desires. Then, jump into action to face your issues and achieve your dreams.

Your time is running out.

Do not delay.

OPPOSITE

Sometimes, delaying is a wise idea.

If you are going to purchase a car or a house, it may be wise to sleep on it overnight. If you are composing a frustrated or angry email to your boss or lover, you may wish to save a draft before sending it, and review it the next day when your emotions have calmed down.

Once again, discernment is a valuable skill in helping you know when to apply this particular life lesson.

You may wish to take your time making big decisions or acting rashly, triggered by intense emotions.

However, when there is a problem that needs addressing, dirty dishes in the sink, or something you know you want out of life, the time to take action is now. Do not delay.

CHAPTER 45

Don't Tell Me What You Can Do, Show Me

This life lesson is self-explanatory.

Talk is cheap, they say.

Actions speak louder than words, they say.

Demonstrate your knowledge and ability through action.

Apply what you know.

No one cares what you say you can do. People care about what you are doing. So stop talking, and get busy doing.

When your actions speak for you, there are few words left to say. You have a tranquil confidence, a peaceful knowing of what you can do, as evidenced by what you have done. Egoic pride and arrogance are unnecessary. There is no need to brag. What you have done and continue to do speaks louder than any verbal proclamation of potential future achievements.

Be skeptical of those who talk a lot about what they can do. That is pride, not confidence. Place your faith in those who demonstrate their capabilities through action, not words. Seek to be such a person yourself.

Trust people who demonstrate what they can do. Gain the confidence and respect of others by demonstrating what you can do. Tell the world what you can do by actually doing it. Talk about it afterwards, if at all.

Consider in your own life, are there things you have spoken of doing, but have not done? It is disempowering to confide your objectives in others, then not follow through. It diffuses your energy, and others lose faith in you. You are weak, and untrustworthy. Conversely, have you ever just gotten up off your butt and gotten something done? It feels empowering, and builds confidence in yourself, and the belief others have in you.

To respect yourself, and earn the respect of others, shut your mouth and take action.

Don't tell me what you can do. Show me.

OPPOSITE

Sometimes you need to tell others what you can do. For instance, in a sales presentation or job interview. Yet, in either case, your past performance is used as evidence of your abilities. Your future performance requires delivering on your promises, or facing the real-world consequences of failure.

Thus, there is no opposite to this life lesson.

Pay attention to people's actions, more so than their words. Watch what they do.

Be someone whose actions match your words. Say less, do more. Demonstrate what you can do through your behaviors, then say nothing at all.

Don't tell me what you can do. Show me.

CHAPTER 46

The Value Of Self-Discipline

When you see someone who is fit, has a thin abdomen, a firm buttocks and well-toned muscles, do you think they got that way by sitting around feeling sorry for themselves, habitually living a sedentary life and eating junk food? Or do you think they consistently exercise self-discipline, when it comes to their habits of diet and exercise?

When you see someone who is wealthy, living in a beautiful home, traveling the world, and enjoying the finer things in life - yes, some folks have it all handed to them – but do you have any idea how hard working, dedicated, committed and self-disciplined most wealthy people are?

When you see a masterful musician or martial artist, there is but one obvious conclusion you can reach about their capacity for self-discipline.

Without self-discipline, your life will never be more than mediocre.

> Either you are living the life
> you want, or you are not.

If you are not living your best life, either accept that you are not, and continue living as you are, or change how you live.

Remember, there are only two ways to make a change: Start, or stop. If you intend for your life to be any better than it is in this moment, then an inherent requirement for this to happen is for you to exercise the self-discipline required to stop what you must stop, and start what you must start. There is no other way.

It is utterly imperative that you develop as much self-discipline as you possibly can, as soon as you possibly can. Then sustain it and apply it, towards the directions you prefer.

Go back to Lesson Number One: Take Care of Yourself First. Practice self-discipline. Take care of your physical, mental, emotional, spiritual and financial health. There is no one else to do it for you.

Do not waste your life away.

Get clear on what is important to you, and have the self-discipline to go after it. Or not. The choice is up to you. What would your ancestors say? What would your higher self say? What would your mother say? What will YOU say, on your death bed?

Cultivate the self-discipline to pursue the life you desire and deserve.

Or not. The choice is up to you.

OPPOSITE

Sometimes it is okay to just relax. Be the imperfect human that you are. Eat that chocolate cake and vanilla ice cream. Sleep in and skip your morning workout. Drink too much wine or whiskey. Get high and take an afternoon nap.

But if you let yourself go too often, your life will slip away, and you will die unfulfilled.

Therefore, there is no opposite to this life lesson that will ever serve you well. Discipline yourself. Allow yourself to be imperfect, yet understand:

You can have results or excuses, but not both.

CHAPTER 47

Excuses Are Like Assholes

Excuses are like assholes: Everyone has them, and they all stink.

Any time anyone presents you with an excuse, you can surmise right away that they are full of shit.

So are you, whenever you make excuses.

Do not make excuses.

For anything.

Ever.

Either you are learning to play the banjo, or you are not.

Either you are practicing karate, or you are not.

The dishes are clean, or they are dirty.

The rent or mortgage is paid, or it is past due.

Either you ran that marathon you kept talking about and training for, or you did not.

Either you quit smoking and lost weight, or you did not.

Regardless of how abusive and negligent your parents and others may have been to you in your formative years, either you have healed your wounds from childhood trauma, or you have not.

Either you pass your unhealed wounds on to others, or you do not.

Either you are being the person that you want to be, or you are not.

Do not tell me what you can do, show me. How you live your life will demonstrate if something is important to you, or not. If you are not focused on something – is it really important to you? Certainly, do not make excuses for why you are not doing it.

Remember, you can have results or excuses, but not both.

OPPOSITE

Reasons are different than excuses. For instance, a single mother working full time while raising children may not have the time or money for banjo lessons and karate class. This could be more so a reason than an excuse.

Under some conditions, perhaps life's limitations and constraints might reasonably prohibit some folks from achieving all they desire.

Reasons are practical, they make sense. Excuses smell like excrement, because they are. If you are honest with yourself, you can usually distinguish between a reason and an excuse.

Since there is a distinction between reasons and excuses, there is no opposite to this life lesson that will serve you well.

Excuses are like assholes: Everyone has them, and they all stink.

Do not make excuses. For anything. Ever.

CHAPTER 48

Give Your Future Self Gifts

Have you ever found money in a pair of pants or the pocket of a jacket that you have not worn in a while?

Have you ever planted a vegetable garden, then months later, savored the fresh, ripe produce straight off the vine?

Have you ever had a little extra money, and enjoyed spending it on yourself, while appreciating the effort that went into acquiring it?

Have you ever saved money for retirement, and you still have it?

Have you ever sown seeds, then reaped the rewards later?

Have you ever delayed your immediate gratification in order to enjoy a greater benefit in the future?

Today, it may be that you do not have everything you want in life, but you can certainly plant a few seeds that will be gifts to your future self.

Forge new relationships and fortify existing ones. Learn new skills, adopt new habits, build your net worth, hide some cash in your winter coat, or literally, plant a vegetable garden.

Eating healthy and exercising are gifts for your future self. Learning valuable skills is a gift for your future self. Kicking bad habits and replacing them with good ones is a gift for your future self. Having a practice and practicing is a gift for your future self.

Imagine if your younger self had given the effort to plant such seeds for you to harvest today. Perhaps you did. Imagine tomorrow, when your future self will receive the benefit of today's planning and concerted effort.

Make a habit of leaving gifts for your future self. Eventually you will reach the point where every day, or at least every so often, you will be enjoying the bountiful harvest of these previously planted gifts.

What gifts can you give to your future self? A bad habit to stop? A good habit to start? A few extra dollars in savings? A new skill to acquire? Getting some exercise? Cleaning your house? Getting a good night's sleep?

Make a habit of planting seeds along your path. Give yourself a gift today that you can harvest tomorrow.

OPPOSITE

Be sure to give yourself some gifts along the way. Do not wait until the very end to reap all of your rewards. While delayed gratification has its merits, remember to enjoy your path as you go.

Another noteworthy opposite arises when you consider that everything you do has impact. Food is medicine, or poison. If the seeds that your habits and lifestyle choices are planting are not gifts to your future self, they may be detriments. You are giving your future self hardships by participating in unwise behaviors today. Consider yourself forewarned!

So, enjoy some of life's pleasures today. Yet, be mindful that everything you do is preparing gifts or troubles for the times ahead. Plant seeds today that will bear the future fruits of good fortune. Give your future self gifts.

CHAPTER 49

Lay The Groundwork

When you build a house, you do not start by placing furniture in a vacant lot, then building the roof above the furniture, followed by the walls beneath the roof, the floor beneath the walls, and finally digging and pouring the foundation beneath the floor.

You start by building a foundation, followed by the floor, then the walls, then the roof. Only when construction is finished is the house furnished.

If you are a land developer, you know that before you dig and pour a foundation, you must lay the groundwork.

Honor the process.

For anything you wish to build or create, you are wise to first lay the groundwork. Establish a strong foundation.

To become a skilled banjo player, start by playing scales and chords, until you know them well. To earn a black belt in karate, start by practicing the basic moves, until they become second nature. To grow vegetables, start with fertile soil.

What do you want to create? What are the first steps? Are you working on something already in process? Do you have a strong foundation?

Whenever you wish to start something new or progress on a current endeavor, remember to lay the groundwork.

What groundwork can you lay today, upon which to build tomorrow?

Laying the groundwork starts with taking care of yourself first. Take care of your health on all levels. Physically, mentally, emotionally, relationally, spiritually and financially.

The only way to make a change is to stop or start something. Stop hurting yourself. Set aside your bad habits. Start cleansing, purifying, and strengthening your body, mind and spirit. Have a practice, and practice, practice, practice. This is laying the groundwork and the foundation upon which to build the rest of your life.

Instead of starting your day by waking up accidentally and making coffee, followed by checking your cell phone, investment portfolio and the world news, do something different. Wake up early, meditate, practice chi gong or yoga, drink some tea or lemon juice, do a few sit ups and pushups, go for a run or to the gym, play the banjo or tuba, read a book, then get to work early, or take deliberate steps towards implementing your next business idea that can lead to your financial freedom. Choose whatever version of this works for you.

Be sure to get sunlight, drink clean water, eat healthy food, and spend time with your favorite people, those who are positive, supportive and encouraging, those who are doing great things with their lives, even if the great things are done in silence and obscurity, even if the great things are simply to be present, kind and loving.

This is the first groundwork to lay, within and around yourself, upon which all else is built.

OPPOSITE

There is absolutely no opposite to this life lesson that will ever serve you well. No matter what you are doing, always remember to lay the groundwork and build a strong foundation. Start with yourself.

CHAPTER 50

Honor The Process

Many an overnight success has toiled relentlessly in anonymity for years, if not decades.

A sapling becomes a mighty tree gradually, muscles build over time.

First you must learn numbers and counting, before learning basic arithmetic. Only then can you progress to algebra and geometry, before proceeding on to trigonometry and calculus.

The first day you pick up the banjo, you will not be a virtuoso. Your first day on the mat in karate class, you will not be a black belt.

You get the point. Growth is a process that requires time, persistence, perseverance and patience.

Be willing to take small steps daily towards the ends you desire. Results may not be immediate.

Yet, the only way you will ever run a marathon is to start by getting comfortable running a kilometer first.

Honor the process. Commit and persevere. Some days will be better than others. Some days you just won't have it in you. Other days you may be surprised at how far you have come by consistently taking small steps.

No matter the process, be it learning a new skill, grieving the loss of a relationship, growing a garden, or anything else, honor the process.

Go one step at a time.

Understand that you will spend time playing scales and chord progressions slowly, before mastering the banjo and joining a bluegrass band.

Understand that you will spend years practicing basic moves on the karate mat, before you are lethally dangerous.

What are you currently working on? Are you studying a musical instrument or martial art? Starting a business? Building a house? Writing a book? Earning a master's degree? Growing a garden? Grieving the loss of a loved one? Discovering your blind spots? Healing your childhood trauma?

Where are you at in your process? What is the next step? Keep the end goal in mind, yet accept where you are at, and realize that all you need to do is take the very next step.

You may also wish to look back, and give yourself some credit, considering how far you have already come.

And since you still have more life left to live, what more might you wish to do? Whether choosing something new, or continuing with what you have already chosen, always remember, it is a process. Begin where you are at. Take small steps as you can. Do not give up. Keep going.

With this in mind, you can achieve great things, as long as you remember to honor the process.

OPPOSITE

There is no opposite to this life lesson that will serve you well. Honor the processes required in life. Go one step at a time, and just keep going.

CHAPTER 51

Finish What You Start

This life lesson needs little explanation.

Finish what you start.

When you leave incompletes lingering in your life, it is an energetic drag on your attention and psyche. It may also leave you with lower self-esteem, because you are someone who does not do what you set out to do. You are not trustworthy. You cannot even rely on yourself.

When you finish what you start, you feel better about yourself than when you have incompletes cluttering up your life. It also frees up your attention and energy to move forward in life, rather than stay stuck.

> Remember, how you practice is how you play, and your life is your practice. So, practice seeing your endeavors through to completion.

When you finish what you start, you will enjoy a sense of satisfaction and fulfillment. You will have an inner knowing and firm confidence that cannot be achieved from outside of yourself.

It will also build the trust and confidence that others have in you, because they see that you follow through your intentions and words with your actions. You are reliable and trustworthy.

If you never complete what you start, you will always be someone who tells people what you can do, rather than showing them.

Think of all the incompletes in your life. Take a moment right now to feel how you will feel when you have completed them. What is the one thing in your life that you have started that will bring you the greatest sense of relief, satisfaction, confidence, peace and well-being when it is finished? Choose one thing. Focus on it. Commit to it. See it through to completion.

Get clear on who you truly are, and what is truly important to you. Go after what you truly desire. Reject other people's limiting beliefs. Don't tell me what you can do, show me. Remember, God rewards action. Do not delay. Make no excuses. Lay the groundwork. Honor the process. AND...

Finish what you start.

OPPOSITE

Perhaps there are extenuating circumstances in life that prohibit you from completing something. Or, half way into an endeavor, you realize it is not the path you wish to pursue. Thus, it may not always be the wisest course of action to finish what you start.

Yet, by keeping this life lesson in mind, you may be more selective about what you choose to start in the first place.

With situational awareness and discernment, you will know when to stop pursuing a path that is no longer in alignment. Otherwise, as a general rule of thumb, this life lesson will serve you well.

Finish what you start.

CHAPTER 52

Choose One Thing

Some folks suggest that multitasking is a myth, and that you can only do one thing at a time. However, a parent might suggest that it is possible to cook dinner, do the laundry, bathe one child, help another with homework and talk on the phone all at the same time.

For the purpose of this life lesson, whether or not multitasking is possible is not the question. The point here is to understand the value of focusing your attention and energy on one thing at a time.

Everyone has a To Do List, if not on paper, at least in their minds.

You have a short-term To Do List comprised of activities that include life maintenance, recreation and personal development. Examples could be going to the market, reading a book or going to the gym.

You also have a long-term To Do List, with objectives that may take weeks, months or years to accomplish. Examples could be to loose ten pounds, grow a vegetable garden or earn a master's degree.

You will die with an unfinished To Do List. However, by choosing one thing at a time, you can achieve amazing results before then.

It can be overwhelming and even immobilizing to look at a lengthy list of everything you want to accomplish, whether they are life maintenance tasks, recreational pursuits or long-term objectives.

For sure, it is wise to have such a list. Write down everything you need to do, and want to do. Then prioritize them chronologically.

Now, here is the key: select the single item at the top of your list, set aside the rest of the list, and focus on that one thing.

Focus your attention and energy on one thing at a time.

Choose one thing on your short-term To Do List, and do that until it is complete, or as far as you can go for the moment. Then choose another. By focusing your attention in this way, you will be able to check numerous items off your short-term To Do List efficiently.

Your long-term To Do List has one or more overarching objectives that are processes. For these items, in each moment, you generally choose one thing within one thing. For instance, if your One Big Thing is to earn a master's degree, then tomorrow, your one thing within one thing may be to read one chapter of one text book for one class.

Perhaps your long-term To Do List includes learning the banjo and karate. You can do both concurrently over a period of time. Yet, in any given moment, you will only be training for one of the two.

The first point here is that in each moment, you are focusing on one thing at a time. So be mindful of what you are choosing to focus on, and give your attention fully to it.

Be fully present with what you are doing.

When you choose to practice the banjo, practice the banjo. When you choose to practice karate, practice karate. This is what it means to choose one thing.

The other part of this lesson is to be clear on what you need to do, and want to do, both short-term and long-term.

You must regularly proceed in accomplishing your short-term tasks. These will change over time, if not daily. You will cross off completed items and add new ones. You will constantly rearrange your list chronologically and by priority.

Then, it is highly advisable to get super duper ultra crystal clear about the overarching theme or themes in your life.

> Choose the One Big Thing that is most important. Then, continuously give all of your attention, intention, focus and energy to that.

For instance, your One Big Thing might be to earn a certain level of income, run a marathon, loose ten pounds, surf tropical beaches, or master the banjo or karate.

Consider now, can you identify your One Big Thing?

Perhaps you have multiple One Big Things that are inter-related and build off each other. Achieving one will help you achieve the rest. Whichever one you believe is the most important, and is the key to unlocking the doors to all the others, choose that One Biggest Thing. Focus your time, energy, attention and intention on this, such that everything else flows naturally from it.

> Choose One Big Thing. Focus on that.
> All the time. No matter what. And… Take Action.

This will produce the most rapid and desirable results, rather than spreading yourself thin over multiple areas. The fewer things you focus on, the more progress you will make.

Finally, remember that everything you do is leading you closer to, or farther away from, your One Big Thing.

Every day, every action you take, you are always choosing one thing. So, be deliberate and intentional, when you make your choices.

OPPOSITE

You can listen to an audiobook while exercising. Thus, you can choose to do two things simultaneously. However, in each moment, you are either focusing on the audiobook while exercising mindlessly, or focusing on your workout, and not absorbing the content of the audiobook. You might alternate your attention between the two, but you are always choosing one thing over the other.

Likewise, over time, you can both earn a black belt in karate and master playing the banjo. You will alternate between practicing one, then the other. Yet, in each moment, you are always choosing one thing at a time.

Furthermore, life continuously requires you to shift the focus of your attention between multiple tasks and objectives. Yet, in each moment, you are always choosing one thing. Thus, there is no practical opposite to this life lesson.

Whether it is your short-term or long-term To Do Lists, whether it is for life maintenance, recreation, personal development or other reasons, be fully present with the task at hand, and set aside everything else.

Over time, you will choose many things, and they will overlap. In any given moment, you are always choosing one thing.

You can efficiently accomplish numerous near-term objectives by approaching them one by one. Then, get crystal clear on the overarching themes of your life. Determine your top priorities. Focus on those with unwavering and relentless persistence and tenacity.

> In every moment, choose one thing.
> Then get it done. No matter what.

CHAPTER 53

Master Something

This life lesson is purely optional. You do not have to master anything in your life. However, if you choose to master something, you will be happy that you did, and it will serve you well.

To master something, you do not have to become famous or the best there ever was. Simply do it until you know it inside and out, it becomes second nature, and you can do complex things with ease. It will be good enough that you know you are a master, and enjoy what you do.

Rich is an electrician who can fix electrical systems that do not work, and build ones that do. He is not a movie star or a guru in white robes. He is a normal man with his joys and sorrows, his dreams and aspirations, his trials and tribulations. Yet, he is an extraordinary man, in many ways. One such way is because he is a master of his craft. He never advertises, because his work speaks for itself. He does not call himself an expert. He simply says, "Yes, I can do that." He will look you squarely in your eyes and shake your hand firmly, then perform his craft with skill and care.

Everyone who hires him is happy with the service they receive in exchange for the price they pay. Rich is a master in plain clothes.

Have you ever met someone who is a master of their craft? You just know it, and they do too.

Have you ever mastered something in your own life? If so, take a moment here to congratulate yourself on what you have accomplished.

Is there something you are currently working on mastering? If so, good for you. Keep it up!

Is there anything else that you would like to master in this lifetime?

Perhaps you wish to master the banjo or karate. You could master gardening, computer programming, or human relationships. You may wish to master your emotions, if they have control over you.

If you so desire, you can become a master. Figure out what is important to you, and choose one thing. Do not delay. God rewards action. Take action today. Honor the process. Just continue taking the next step until you have mastered something, if you so choose.

The most advanced application of this life lesson is to master yourself.

This may take a superhuman effort. Most people will never master themselves. Yet, some do, and so can you, if you so choose.

What would it look like, to master yourself? What might it feel like, to master yourself? Close your eyes and go there for a moment. Welcome back. How was that?

Perhaps you are already well on your way to self-mastery. Perhaps the idea is daunting, or of no interest to you. That is fine too. This life lesson is purely optional.

In case the possibility intrigues you, here are some visions of what self-mastery may look like:

Controlling your thoughts, rather than allowing them to control you.

Controlling your emotions, rather than allowing them to control you.

Healing your traumas, so they no longer control you.

Becoming self-aware, shedding light on your blind spots, knowing your wounds and triggers, regulating your nervous system so you can stay present with your triggers, and transforming unconscious reactivity into conscious responsiveness.

Remaining calm under pressure and in stressful situations.

Having the confidence and ability to handle anything that confronts you.

Behaving wisely in each moment

Living a lifestyle where you are cleansing, purifying and strengthening your body, mind and spirit through your daily behaviors and habits.

Eating food that is medicine, rather than poison.

Exercising regularly.

Abstaining from drugs, alcohol and other forms of self-destruction.

Having a practice, and practicing regularly.

Mastering a musical instrument or martial art, or something similar that that ignites your passion and drive.

Mastering your finances. Being debt-free, living frugally, earning more than you spend, investing wisely and building your net worth. Having enough money to survive and thrive, to help other people, and to build your own empire.

Mastering the art of human relationships. Learning to communicate clearly, directly, authentically and skillfully. Allowing people to be as they are, without judgment or condemnation. Giving people the gift of being seen and heard, acknowledged and validated.

Being peaceful, calm, present and confident.

Knowing that you are good enough, as you are.

Developing a trustworthy character. Being someone other people know they can rely upon. Showing what you can do, rather than talking about it. Matching your actions to your words. Keeping your agreements. Being up front with your transactions. Accepting no bullshit, ever.

Self-mastery sounds a lot like true freedom, does it not?

It also sounds a lot like applying the lessons in this book.

Now, cut yourself some slack if you are only half-way there. The author ain't perfect either. In fact, no one is.

Most humans do not master themselves. You can choose to master something more specific, the banjo, or karate, for instance. Yet keep in mind, the ultimate mastery is of the self.

Honor the process, just take one step closer every day.

Consider mastering something. Choose one thing, do not delay, start today, practice, practice, practice, and eventually you will become a master.

OPPOSITE

There is no opposite to this life lesson that will serve you well.

Mastery is optional. Self-mastery is the ultimate mastery. You do not have to master anything. If you choose to, master something. Consider mastering yourself, or at least taking steps in that direction. God rewards action, so do not delay.

CHAPTER 54

Be Curious

Have you ever met someone who thinks they know everything? Boring, right? No room for growth or improvement. You cannot have a conversation to explore new possibilities with them.

Have you ever been disinterested in all of life? Depressing, right? No room for awe, excitement or adventure.

The antidote to thinking you know everything, or to being disinterested in life, is to be curious.

Approach life, people and the world with curiosity.

This life lesson is founded on the primary importance of awareness. To approach life with curiosity is to apply your awareness, engage in what is happening, enliven the present moment.

> When you wake up in the morning,
> say to yourself, "I look forward
> to seeing how life unfolds today."

When you interact with another human being, be curious. Who is this person? What is their knowledge, experience and perspective? What is their wisdom? What are their joys and sorrows?

Every person you meet has a unique world view and set of life experiences. Most have an inner life as rich and complex as your own. Not only will you hear wild stories and learn new things by being curious about other people, but you will make new friends and enjoy abundant connection everywhere you go.

Being curious about other people will also help you develop compassion, because you will find that people are mostly the same, and everyone has their struggles.

Also be curious about the natural world. Enjoy the beauty of a colorful rainbow, delight in the scent of a fragrant flower. Add texture and depth to your life, enrich your moment-by-moment experiences.

> Around every bend in your path
> awaits a new surprise, a new adventure.

Being curious opens you to greater possibilities for experience. Are you curious about all the hidden secrets that await you? Are you ready for life to become an adventure of discovery?

When you approach life with cynicism, or the belief that you already know everything, you cut yourself off from the wonders of creation that surround you, and from connection with other people. Is that how you want to live?

Everyone you encounter has something to teach you, life experiences to share, and a connection to enjoy.

Every city block you turn the corner, new curiosities await.

Live as if life were an experiment, an adventure, a discovery, a dream.

> Want to know what happens next. Be curious.

OPPOSITE

There may be wise limits to your curiosity. If you are curious to know if you can fly, start by jumping off a small cliff, rather than a large one. If you are curious to learn about electricity, perhaps sticking a metal fork into an electrical outlet is not the best way to satisfy that curiosity.

Furthermore, there are times when you may need to retreat from life, to turn inward, to have a quiet and calm environment. After venturing outside your comfort zone, your nervous system will benefit from retreating back into a safe and comfortable space.

Sometimes, it is okay to not be curious, just relax, and give yourself a break. Snuggle up with what is familiar.

Yet, as a general rule of thumb, be curious, at least some of the time. Be curious about specific subjects that fascinate you. Be curious about life, other people and the world. You will find countless wonders and surprises along your way.

CHAPTER 55

Say Thank You

Often, you do not appreciate what you have until it is gone.

Remember to appreciate what you have while you still have it. Count your blessings, and take a moment to be grateful for them.

In modern spiritual movements, the whole "attitude of gratitude" thing is a bit tiresome and worn out. However, there is some basic truth to it.

Sure, sometimes life sucks. Sometimes a little, sometimes a lot. Some folks get dealt a particularly shitty hand, while others seem to have all the luck.

However, there is usually something for which you can be grateful, no matter the difficulties and tragedies you encounter. Some folks even suggest that developing genuine gratitude in your heart is a way to invite more things into your life for which to be grateful.

See how it works for you.

Take a moment right now to consider everything in your life for which you can be grateful. Seriously, do this right now, and see how you feel afterwards.

Next, take a pen and paper, and write down twenty things you are fortunate to have in your life. Spend a moment to appreciate how each one enhances your life.

Remember to appreciate other people. Your friends and partner if you have one. Those you work with. Your customers, neighbors and service providers. Perhaps even your family members. If you have food, shelter and good company, appreciate these things too.

Now, don't overdo it. Being overly appreciative is obnoxious and inauthentic. Don't force it. When your neighbor collects your mail while you are on vacation, a box of chocolates as gratitude will suffice. When your company achieves its sales goals a small bonus for your employees will suffice.

Remember to be grateful to yourself as well. You have probably been through a lot, exerted extraordinary efforts over the years, suffered setbacks, heartbreaks, loss and grief, and kept on going.

Remember to appreciate yourself, the people around you, and all of your good fortune, even if sometimes life really sucks.

A simple and effective way to apply this life lesson is to appreciate the food you have to eat by reciting this prayer before a meal:

"For that which I am about to receive, let me be truly grateful. Amen."

When you are sharing a meal with others, you can share this prayer with them as well:

"For that which we are about to receive, let us be truly grateful. Amen."

In general, remember to be grateful for the people in your life, those who serve you, those who keep you company, and those who do kind things for you. Be grateful for that which you have: food, shelter, warmth, dryness. You can only focus on one thing at a time, so when you are focused on appreciation, there is no room to feel negatively. Furthermore, it could be that when you are focusing on your good fortune, you are inviting greater fortune into your life.

This is a simple life lesson: Remember to say thank you.

OPPOSITE

There may be people in your life who like to treat you abusively. But they do nice things for you too, so they may feel justified in their abusive treatment of you. For instance, this could be a parent, spouse, sibling, friend or employer.

If someone treats you poorly, and justifies it because they do nice things for you, you do not need to be grateful to them. However, you can still be grateful for the nice things.

If someone holds you hostage, but feeds you, you do not need to be grateful to them for providing you with food and shelter. However, you could still be grateful for the food and shelter, just not for the people.

Aside from hypothetical situations with abusive people and whatnot, it is usually a good idea to be grateful. Practice genuine appreciation for all that you have in life.

Practice saying thank you.

CHAPTER 56

No Bullshit. Ever.

What bullshit do you tolerate in your life? Do you bullshit yourself? Do you bullshit other people? Do you allow other people to bullshit you?

Choose to live a life of honesty, authenticity, integrity and truth.

First, take a look within. How do you bullshit yourself?

This is about being honest with yourself. It falls under the umbrella of shedding light on what is dark and getting to know your blind spots. Everyone wants to believe they are decent human beings, even with their faults. What will set you apart from others is if you are actually willing to look at your faults and imperfections, your blind spots, your dark side. Be honest with yourself about your shortcomings, do not bullshit yourself.

If one person calls you a jerk, it could be them. If three people call you a jerk, it is probably you. Are you a jerk?

How do you lie to yourself? About what are you are in denial? What secrets are you keeping from yourself?

"I do not have a drug or alcohol problem. I could quit if I wanted to."

"Even though my spouse is abusive, I am better staying than leaving."

"Even though I hate my job, it is worth it to work 50 hours a week, 50 weeks a year for 50 years, so I can go to the dog park on the weekends, then spend a few years in retirement, old and decrepit, sleeping in and watching daytime television before I die."

"Other people's politicians are self-interested, self-serving, manipulative, misleading, dishonest, corrupt, fraudulent and heartless, but the politicians that I support are honest, incorruptible and altruistic – my politicians really care."

"If I ignore the problem, it will go away."

You get the idea. These are the kinds of lies people tell themselves. What lies do you tell yourself? Notice how you bullshit yourself, then stop.

Do not bullshit yourself. Ever. Be honest with yourself about everything.

Second, do not bullshit other people.

Be upfront with your transactions. Be direct in your communication. Live with integrity, have a trustworthy character, match your actions to your words, do what you say you are going to do, when you say you are going to do it. Keep your agreements, and when you cannot, renegotiate them.

Do not lie, cheat or steal. Look people directly into their eyes, shake their hands firmly, tell the truth and shoot straight.

To not bullshit other people also means to be your authentic self, rather than being someone you are not, in order to gain acceptance or approval. Do not change who you are to please other people. Do not pretend to be anything other than that which you are.

Third, no bullshit means do not accept bullshit from other people.

Some people are full of shit. Other people are simply that which they present themselves to be, what you see is what you get. Most people are somewhere in between.

If someone is dishonest, disallow them from your life. If someone is abusive, disallow them from your life. If someone discourages you, puts you down, invalidates you or treats you like a worthless piece of shit in any way whatsoever, disallow them from your life. And do not do such things to other people.

How do you show up in the world? Full of shit, totally authentic, or somewhere in between? Can you notice how others show up?

Develop the ability to read other people's energies and characters. What kind of "vibes" are they exuding? Do their actions match their words? Are their personalities accurate representations of their characters? Are they reliable and trustworthy? Or are they full of shit?

It can be difficult, and perhaps unwise, to directly confront people when they are bullshitting you. Their defenses go up, and they are unwilling to hear about their shortcomings. It is rare to find folks who will genuinely accept such feedback. However, you can certainly notice when other folks are out of alignment, inauthentic, or bullshitting you, and navigate your life and your relationships with them accordingly.

Stop bullshitting yourself. Stop bullshitting others. Do not allow others to bullshit you, or at least recognize when they do, and be on guard against it. Shoot straight, and align yourself with others who shoot straight too. Do not allow bullshit in your life.

OPPOSITE

Politics is full of bullshit. The news is full of bullshit. Your work place may be full of bullshit. Your family dynamic may be full of bullshit. You may need to lie to a bad person to escape a difficult or dangerous situation. These are the realities of life.

Yet, within your own domain, as a general rule of thumb, live your life by this rule: No Bullshit. Teach by your way of being. Observe the characters of others. Demand integrity from yourself and in others. Tolerate no bullshit. See who shows up, who sticks around, and who falls away.

CHAPTER 57

Keep Your Agreements

This life lesson is a cousin to many others. Develop a trustworthy character. Live with integrity. Tolerate no bullshit. Do what you say you will do. Match your actions to your words. Keep your agreements.

First, keep your agreements with yourself.

When you commit to doing something for yourself, do it. This can only build your confidence and belief in yourself. If you do not keep your agreements with yourself, it may erode your self-esteem. If you always commit to achieving the impossible, you will always let yourself down. Be selective in the agreements you do make, and perhaps start small. Practice making modest agreements with yourself and keeping them. This will build your habit of following through on what you set out to do.

Now, consider the possibility of making a large and important agreement with yourself. It could even be your One Big Thing. Then keep it. No matter what. See how THAT makes you feel.

Next, keep your agreements with other people.

When you make an agreement with someone else, look them squarely in the eyes, shake their hand firmly, commit to doing what you say you will do, and then do it.

If, after making the agreement, you realize you cannot keep it, or do not want to, then communicate this, and either cancel or renegotiate it.

Have you ever noticed that often the best business deals are handshake agreements? Both parties trust each other, and they trust themselves. They do what they have agreed to do.

Have you ever noticed how rare these relationships are?

Usually, people need contracts. For borrowing money, buying a car or a house, for construction projects, for marriage! Yes, getting things in writing is a good idea.

Yet, when you find folks who honor handshake agreements, keep them close to you. Be such a person too.

If you agree to be in a committed monogamous relationship, do not cheat. Easier said than done. This is where the no bullshit rule comes into play. Be honest with your partner, and yourself. Good luck with that!

> When you keep your agreements, people notice. They respect and trust you, because your actions match your words.

You will be known and respected as an honorable person. Your friends, family and associates will know that they can count on you. You are reliable. You are trustworthy.

Consider in your own life, what kind of people you know. Do you know folks who will commit to attending the dinner party you are hosting on Friday night, and then simply not show up? Do you know other folks who will be there Friday night without a doubt, because they gave you their word?

Which kind of person are you?

A corollary here is to be judicious in the agreements that you do choose to make. Make agreements sparingly, rather than casually, and only when you are certain that you can and want to keep them.

Consider being someone who always keeps your agreements. Imagine how it feels to be such a person. Imagine how other people perceive you. You are responsible. You are respectable. You are reliable. You are trustworthy. You can be counted on. You have a sound character. You are confident, and believe in yourself, because you are who you say you are, and you do what you say you will do.

Be trustworthy and reliable.

Keep your agreements.

OPPOSITE

You may not be able to keep all of your agreements. Forgive yourself. Do your best.

If you can, cancel or renegotiate an agreement you have made that you cannot or do not want to honor.

While there may be some exceptions to this general rule of thumb, there is absolutely no opposite to this life lesson that will ever serve you well. Whenever possible, if not at all times, keep your agreements.

PART EIGHT

Your Health

CHAPTER 58

Your Health Is Of Primary Importance

Always value the importance of your health. Make it a top priority. Take care of yourself first. Start by taking care of your body. This is the number one act of personal responsibility. A wise person makes this their first intention and focus. A practical person does too.

You may not value your health until it is gone. Most folks take it for granted that they can walk, run, see, hear, smell, lie down, sit up, chew, swallow and digest food and excrete the waste. Until they cannot.

You tend to not notice your body when it is functioning properly. Yet, when it is not, you can hardly notice anything else at all.

How often do people undervalue their health? Quite frequently. It is well known that smoking, drinking and junk food are bad for human health. Nonetheless, people smoke, drink and eat junk food all the time.

> Every one of your behaviors is supporting your health, or not.

Everything you eat has healing or harmful properties, perhaps some of each. Every action you take strengthens your health, or weakens it, even if but by imperceptible increments.

The human body is quite miraculous. It can withstand and heal from significant amounts of abuse. But one day, your bad habits will catch up to you. That day, and the days that follow, may be full of regret for all the times you abused your health but your body tolerated it.

Your health is of paramount importance. Always value your health. In everything that you do. This cannot be emphasized enough.

Whenever you are sick or immobile, you will remember this life lesson. Do not wait until you have lost your health before you understand its importance and implement it in your life.

Your mental and emotional health are as important as your physical health.

Are you surrounded by negative and toxic people? Or by positive, uplifting, encouraging and supportive people?

Do you take some time to do the things you love to do?

Do you cultivate loving relationships with those around you?

Can you find peace and calm, or are you always anxious and stressed out?

Consider that your environment, surroundings, behaviors, habits and even thoughts and feelings all influence your health.

Always be mindful of what in your life is supporting your health, and what is detracting from it.

What lifestyle habits do you have that support your health? Which ones do not? What choices do you make that fortify or erode your health?

What can you do today to take better care of your health? Remember, the only two ways to make a change are to start or stop something.

What can you stop doing that will benefit your health? What can you start doing that will benefit your health? The choices are yours.

You do not have to do anything in life, other than die, perhaps pay taxes, and, according to Buddha, experience pain. Everything else is optional.

Do yourself a favor, give your future self gifts, take care of yourself first, and start by taking care of your health. Take your vitamins, floss and brush your teeth, drink clean water, exercise regularly, get fresh air and sunlight, eat healthy food, avoid toxic food, avoid toxic people, do what you love to do, and be sure to cultivate and enjoy loving relationships with those around you, for your mental and emotional health.

Your health is of primary importance. If you neglect your health, you will come to regret it. This is not a threat, it is a promise.

OPPOSITE

There is absolutely no opposite to this life lesson that will ever serve you well.

CHAPTER 59

Exercise Regularly

If you can, exercise. Regularly. It is good for your physical, mental and emotional health.

They say that exercise is the best cure for depression. To say "the best" is a grand statement. However, it sure does help. No matter how you are feeling in any given moment, exercise will most likely make you feel better.

Even walking is great exercise. Some folks say it is one of the best exercises there is. Other folks like to swim in the ocean, climb mountains, run marathons, lift weights or simply practice yoga and chi gong. Choose what exercise works for you, then do it. Regularly.

Do not make excuses for not exercising. Remember, excuses are like assholes, everyone has them, and they all stink.

Now, some folks may have physical handicaps, or even lack arms or legs. They may have legitimate reasons for not being able to exercise. A reason is different than an excuse. If you are so fortunate as to have arms, legs, eyes and ears that all function, then be grateful for these amazing gifts, and put them to use.

Exercise your body.

Exercise your mind, too.

Your brain is like a muscle: a mind unexercised will atrophy. A mind well exercised may stay strong well into old age.

There are countless ways to exercise your mind. Read books. Play music. Have philosophical discussions with friends. Learn new subjects or skills. Build or create things. Solve puzzles.

How do you enjoy exercising your mind? Are you learning new things? Are you creating? If you are reading this book, you probably enjoy exercising your mind. Good for you, keep it up!

Make a habit out of exercising your body and your mind.

OPPOSITE

It is a good idea to take days of rest between days of exercise, to let your body recover. However, you can only take a day off from exercise if you have been exercising. Therefore, there is no opposite to this life lesson that will serve you well.

Exercise your body. Exercise your mind.

CHAPTER 60

Food Is Medicine

Food is medicine. Or poison.

Consider that everything you eat and drink is either making you more healthy or less healthy. The changes are incremental, and usually imperceptible on a daily basis. However, everything registers. Everything has impact. It all adds up over time.

Some folks suggest that you take on the energy embodied in the food you eat, not just chemically, but metaphysically too. Whether it is the suffering of an animal that endured inhumane living conditions before a brutal slaughter, or a fruit that sat peacefully on its tree, basking in gentle sunlight, before its harvest.

The foods you eat are the building blocks for what you become. Every meal creates health or disease. Perhaps you have heard stories of people who cured themselves of terminal illnesses through plant-based diets. Perhaps you have heard stories of people developing diabetes or heart disease as a consequence of unhealthy dietary habits.

Perhaps you are a proponent of organic foods, versus foods grown with toxic chemicals designed in a laboratory for the purpose of destroying life but preserving the crop, or perhaps you do not give much thought to the chemical or metaphysical qualities of your food.

Nonetheless, for thousands of years, people have used food as medicine. Your ancestors did not have pharmacies. They had a deep knowledge of which plants and animals to eat, when and how to eat them, and in what conditions.

Today, there are countless dietary trends and options, each with numerous opinions about their benefits and drawbacks. You will have to find what works for you.

The point here is to be mindful of the food you eat. Remember that everything you put into your body is contributing to your health or your sickness, even if the impact of a single meal is too small to notice.

Whether it is chicken soup to combat the flu, carrots for better eyesight or an organic raw vegan diet to combat cancer, there are countless anecdotal references to food as medicine. If you prefer scientific evidence, you can search the internet and start learning about the vitamins and minerals that food delivers to your body, as well as the toxic and inflammatory properties of some things you ingest.

Food is preventative medicine. Food is curative medicine. Or, food is poison.

OPPOSITE

Sometimes, food is medicine for the soul. Eat that box of cookies, or pint of ice cream to soothe your worried mind or broken heart, if you must. It can help take the edge off of a distressful moment. Yet, understand that this is but a temporary distraction from the pain of existence, and has long-term adverse consequences.

Remember, the nutrient value and embodied energy of your food will, in the long run, do more for you than the temporary satisfaction of your sense pleasures and distraction from the agony of being present with your feelings.

Do yourself a favor, take care of your health, give your future self gifts, and remember, food is medicine, or poison.

CHAPTER 61

The Best Drugs Are The Ones Your Body Creates

Ingesting foreign substances to induce feelings of well-being and altered states of consciousness may be as old as human existence itself. There may be nothing inherently wrong with this.

However, the best drugs are not the ones you put into your body. Rather, the best drugs – usually – are the ones your own body creates.

Most folks do not want to hear this. But the truth does not care about your preferences.

It is easier to lick a toad, eat some fungus, pop a pill, smoke a flower, or sip a beverage from the jungle, laboratory, or cellar, than it is to get your body's own chemical factory producing the best drugs on earth. The latter requires more time and greater effort.

To illustrate the power of the body's drug factory, consider how it is said that gambling is more addictive than heroin. Doing heroin requires introducing a foreign substance to your body. Gambling causes your own body to create the drugs that get you high.

Some folks will insist that certain ingested substances are not drugs, they are "medicines". Get over this point right now. Drug, medicine, chemical, molecule, call it what you will. The body creates chemicals – drugs – that can make you feel absolutely amazing.

Foreign substances introduced to your body connect to the same neural receptors that already exist in your brain. These foreign substances mimic the action of the chemicals – drugs – that your body creates.

It can be argued that if God, The Universe, or whatever creative force there is that caused you to exist, designed your brain with receptors for these foreign substances, then it is perfectly natural to do drugs sourced from outside of your body. This may be so.

However, it may also be that your body has these neural receptors in place because you yourself can produce the chemicals that fit into them.

The difference is that external drugs are fast-acting, and feel great initially. In contrast, you must put in some effort to get your body's drug factory producing, but the feelings of well-being will last longer.

Consider someone who smokes pot and drinks whiskey all day. Then consider someone who starts each morning with meditation, followed by rigorous exercise. Who is enjoying better drugs?

The chemicals your body creates when you experience exercise, sex, falling in love, yoga, meditation, prayer, dancing, singing, and other such activities, bring feelings of happiness, joy, peace and well-being. These types of experiences induce your body into producing the best drugs.

If you want to feel truly amazing, stop doing drugs, and start making your own. What can you do today, and moving forward in your life, to help your body's own drug factory kick into high gear? What can you do to Say Yes To Drugs, your own drugs?

Here are some hints: Start eating healthy, exercising, and practicing meditation, yoga, chi gong and Cobra Breath. Have meaningful pursuits and fulfilling relationships. Have sex regularly, and discover what other activities make you feel amazing naturally. You can take it from there.

OPPOSITE

God did not create plant medicines and chemical drugs if God did not want you to experience them. Foreign substances introduced to your body can swing wide open the doors of perception and assist you in achieving states of consciousness that you might otherwise never attain.

People often have mind-expanding, heart-opening, life-changing experiences due to drugs. With a supportive set and setting, certain substances can be used to heal grief and emotional pain, expand your awareness and enhance your capacity to love.

However, what these experiences do is give you a glimpse of a different or greater reality that you then must access in your everyday sober life, not by constantly doing more drugs.

Furthermore, consider that drugs, including the "sacred medicines", are not for everyone. They cause some people to have very dark experiences that are not therapeutic, and that can even be damaging.

If you are called to explore the outer realms of human consciousness and the inner realms of your own soul and psyche, or simply to escape the sober pain of existence and feel good for a moment, by way of ingesting foreign substances, well, good luck with that.

However, it will serve you well in life to do what you can to enjoy the drugs your body makes naturally, most, if not all of the time.

The best drugs are the ones your body creates.

PART NINE

Healing

CHAPTER 62

Hurt People Hurt People

Everyone has pain in their hearts. Some more so than others.

Furthermore, everyone has a unique temperament – that is, a varying ability to skillfully handle the challenges of life. Some folks are sensitive, and the slightest disturbance can be devastating. Others are more thick-skinned and resilient. They are less affected by potentially traumatic events. Thus, the impact of difficult life experiences varies from person to person.

All things considered, most, if not all people have some amount of pain in their hearts. Some can manage or overcome it with relative ease, while others have greater difficulty or even block it out. Often, people are unconscious of the pain they carry.

When you are not aware of what hurts you, or are unwilling to face it, there is a good chance that you will pass it on to other people without even knowing that you are doing so. You may also find that other people do the same to you.

This is called the perpetuation of the trauma cycle. When people have been hurt, they tend to hurt others in the same or similar manner to how they were hurt. It happens all the time.

Imagine how many generations of humanity this cycle extends back in time.

If a child grew up with abusive parents, that child is prone to become an abusive adult. If your parents frequently invalidated you as a young child, you may develop the subconscious habit of invalidating others.

Sometimes it can be obvious how a person takes out their unhealed wounds onto others. Often, it is subtle.

Consider, for instance, the man who grew up in a "normal" family. However, his parents habitually invalidated him, treating him as though he had no intrinsic value. He grows up, gets married, and has children. He habitually invalidates his wife and children, treating them as if they have no inherent worth. This is a subtle and insidious form of abuse. He does not hit them. He is not an alcoholic. Nonetheless, he unconsciously acts out the hurtful behavior he received, the unhealed pain in his heart, onto his family. He treats his wife and children like worthless pieces of shit, because that is how he learned to treat people, by how his parents treated him. He is not even aware he is doing this, it is automatic. His children then go through life treating others the same way, without realizing they are doing so – their friends, partners, children, even themselves. And so on.

> The cycles of abusive behavior continue, from one generation to the next, until someone becomes aware of it, and chooses to stop passing on the abuse they received.

There are infinite variations on this theme. The point is, people tend to perpetuate the cycle of trauma by treating others hurtfully, as they learned to do by how they have been treated. This is neither conscious nor malicious. They are not intentionally hurting others.

> It is a subconscious behavior.
> People act out the abuse they know. They learn to treat others by how they were treated.

Consider for yourself, how did you learn to treat people? Were you treated hurtfully in your formative years? Did you internalize it? What unhealed pain do you carry in your heart? How do you unconsciously pass it on to others?

This goes back to shedding light on what is dark, discovering your blind spots, and becoming more self-aware. You will need courage and honesty to explore this darkness. For some people this is not a problem. For others, you may be surprised and saddened to realize how you unconsciously take your pain out on other people. Others of you will refuse to acknowledge that you do so, and will go to your graves without the awareness that you are a hurt person hurting other people.

However, if you wish to be a decent human being, it is helpful to remember that hurt people hurt people. When others act hurtfully towards you, realize that they are probably treating you the same way that others treated them, or as a byproduct thereof.

It is also wise to know yourself, and be mindful of how you may be unconsciously passing on the unhealed wounds you carry.

Hurt people hurt people, and this cycle perpetuates itself, throughout human history, until you choose to stop it.

OPPOSITE

Sometimes, someone can have pain in their hearts, yet not pass it on to others. This generally requires an awareness of that pain, and a deliberate intention to not pass it on.

It is said that free people free people, safe people shelter people, enlightened people illuminate people, loving people love people, healed people heal people . . . and hurt people hurt people. Cultivate within yourself that which you wish to pass on to others, and clean up that which you do not.

Hurt people hurt people, until they become aware of it, and choose to stop.

CHAPTER 63

Become Aware Of Your Traumas

This life lesson is a vital step in a series of lessons that begins with shedding light on what is dark, continues with understanding that hurt people hurt people, and then arrives here. Now, it is time to become aware of your own traumas, the unresolved pain in your own heart.

You have an opportunity in this lifetime to become aware of yourself. In fact, some folks suggest that all of life is the process of pure consciousness materializing into physical form for the purpose of knowing itself. Regardless of the source of your being, you are here. Take this time to get to know yourself.

> Some of the most important work you
> can do is to become aware of yourself,
> including your traumas, so you can face them,
> and stop passing them on to other people.

It is up to YOU to cease the perpetuation of the trauma cycle. This is done by becoming aware of your traumas.

Some say it is difficult, if not impossible, to heal all traumas. This may be true. However, you can at least become aware of your wounds, choose to stop unconsciously passing them on, and make an effort to heal what you can. Thus, it is within the realm of possibilities to become a more present, loving, peaceful, calm and well-integrated human being.

Are you aware of your traumas? Perhaps you had perfect parents and an easy life, experiencing and navigating human relationships harmoniously and unscathed by abusive treatment from others. For most people, there is some pain you carry. Become aware of it, so you can be sure not to take it out on other people.

OPPOSITE

Be careful about spending too much time focusing on who has hurt you and how. This can lead to making excuses for staying stuck in unhealthy patterns that do not serve you and justifying your irresponsible behavior because of what others have done to you.

You can spend years in therapy talking about your traumas, yet never make progress in healing them. What you focus on grows. Thus, while it is wise to know the pain in your heart so you can stop passing it on, you are also wise to focus your attention on constructive ways of dealing with it, rather than staying stuck in it.

Therefore, there is no direct opposite to this life lesson. Become aware of your traumas. Then, focus on the resolutions, rather than the causes.

CHAPTER 64

What Happened To You Is Not Your Fault, But It Is Your Responsibility

Understand the pain in your heart, and how it came to be there. Yet, realize that if you continue to focus on the causes of what hurt you, it can lead to self-pity, blaming others for what they did to you, and being stuck in counterproductive patterns of thoughts, feelings and behaviors.

Instead, choose to be proactive about your responses, and the solutions.

It is not your fault that people have behaved hurtfully towards you, unconsciously taking out their unhealed traumas upon you.

However, it IS your responsibility. Whether or not you chose to be born, you are here. And no one is coming to save you from yourself.

It is your responsibility how you react to everything in your life. You can take things personally, you can blame and resent other people, you can stay stuck, unhappy and unfulfilled, or you can realize that when people act hurtfully towards you, it is because of their own pain.

You can choose to confront and overcome your traumas – at least to some extent – in order to live a more peaceful and fulfilling life. What happened to you has happened. Now, YOU decide what to do about it. You can take charge and respond constructively, or let it overwhelm you.

You can unconsciously take your wounds out on other people. You can drown your pain through escapism. You can pretend the pain does not exist. You can engage in countless distractions to keep from being present with yourself and your pain.

Or, you can face it.

You are not responsible for what happened to you. However, you need to take ownership for how you have reacted to it thus far in your life, and how you will respond to it moving forward. Understandably, the pain can be soul crushing and immobilizing. You can allow it to break you, or you can break free from it. In theory, the choice is yours.

No one is coming to save you. There may be others who will guide you along your path, but ultimately, your life is in your own hands.

What happened to you is not your fault, but it is your responsibility.

OPPOSITE

There is no exact opposite to this life lesson. You and you alone are responsible for how you respond to life. Yet, you can enroll the support of others.

Humans need other humans. Healing happens best in community. It is wise to ask for and receive support. It is also one of the greatest gifts you can give, to support those in need. Sometimes, the love of another is the best medicine. So, you do not have to heal all alone, you can certainly ask for help.

However, as a general rule of thumb, the fact remains, what happened to you is not your fault, but it is your responsibility. No one is to blame. No one is coming to save you. You need to leverage all the opportunities before you for salvation, with determination, grit, tenacity and perseverance, to own your shit. It is your choice, how you respond to what has happened to you.

CHAPTER 65

Heal Your Wounds

After shedding light on what is dark by becoming aware of your blind spots, recognizing that hurt people hurt people, becoming aware of your traumas, and realizing that what happened to you is not your fault but it is your responsibility, now you arrive here. It is time to heal your wounds.

Throughout history, much of human experience has been brutal. Trauma has been passed on from one generation to the next, since the beginning of time. It continues today, between individuals, amongst families and within entire societies.

There may be no work more important than the healing of trauma. It starts with you. If you do not heal, you will probably take your pain out unconsciously on other people, especially the ones you love.

It is up to YOU to cease the perpetuation of the trauma cycle.

The healing of trauma is a vast and complex subject beyond the scope of this book. If you feel you need serious trauma healing, then please, seek professional help.

The point here is to be honest with yourself about the wounds you carry, and make the conscious decision to not pass them on to others.

Then, decide to do what it takes to heal. The life lessons in this book will support you on that journey, if you internalize and apply them. Cultivate awareness and compassion, confront your traumas, take care of yourself, and connect with others in healthy and constructive ways.

Some folks suggest that total healing is an impossible task, and that you will always carry some of the grief, self-doubt and pain that you have accumulated in your life. Yet, it is certainly possible to soften the sting of that pain, and heal to some extent, if not completely.

When you become aware of your wounds, choose to not pass them on, and commit to a healing path, you will find your way.

> The destination is peace. The
> tools are awareness and compassion.
> The path is learning, discipline and practice.

The purpose is knowledge of self and connection with others. The journey is learning life's lessons and applying what you learn. The alchemy is transforming pain into peace, if not joy. Humans may be meant to struggle, in order to learn and to grow. Humans are also meant to experience fun, pleasure, laughter, happiness, joy, ecstasy, euphoria, bliss, peace and mind blowing orgasms.

Discover what hurts within you. Choose to not pass it on, and commit to healing your wounds, as best as you can, to play your part in healing your ancestors, your descendants and all of humanity. Earn your birthright to peace and joy. Give yourself the life you deserve. There is no greater work for you to do. God rewards action, so do not delay. What can you do to get started today?

OPPOSITE

There is no opposite to this life lesson that will ever serve you well.

CHAPTER 66

The Only Way Past Is Through

Some folks spend their whole lives unaware of the pain in their hearts. Some folks spend their whole lives escaping that pain. Others become aware of it, and do what it takes to move through it.

Anything can be a distraction. Food, sex, drugs, alcohol, work, money, travel, consumerism, entertainment and social media can all be used as distractions to cover up the pain of existence. None of these things are inherently good or bad. They can be used constructively, or as forms of escapism. The key here is to be mindful how you use them.

No amount of avoidance, denial or escapism will help you overcome your pain. So long as you are not confronting it, it will persist, like a thorn in your side, causing perpetual discomfort.

Numerous wisdom teachings suggest that you must face your pain directly. Acknowledge it, sit with it, and feel it, so you can heal it. Consider that you must go through it to get to the other side. Only then will you be able to let it go, leave it behind, move on and live more fully. The only way past is through.

Now, some folks perpetually attend personal growth workshops full of intellectual ideas on how to overcome themselves, without ever truly confronting their emotional pain. Others spend years in talk therapy, repeatedly reliving their painful experiences, without ever making much progress. The idea here is not to get stuck in your pain, but rather to face it with candor and courage, so you can move beyond it.

Ask yourself, do you have wounds you avoid acknowledging and confronting? What are your preferred methods of escapism? When you stop escaping, what do you really need? A warm room, dry clothes, a bowl of soup, and a place to lay your head at night. Perhaps some good company, physical touch and a glass of water.

> When you stop escaping, what do you feel?
> To actually face yourself can be terrifying,
> if not extremely uncomfortable, at the very least.

If the only way past is through, this means no escapism. At least for a moment in time. Just sit there. Just be. Feel it. All of it. Perhaps then, you can open up the possibility of getting past it, to the other side. Stop distracting yourself. Stop making excuses. Eliminate escapism and feel it all, for a moment. This might be terrible advice, because so many people have such deep pain that to feel it all will cause them to go crazy or kill themselves. You need to be the judge of that for yourself.

If you have the courage, face it, go through it, and get past it.

OPPOSITE

There are schools of sudden enlightenment. Perhaps you can experience breakthroughs with entheogens, healers, breathwork, laughter therapy or tapping, also known as Thought Field Therapy or Emotional Freedom Technique, for example. Perhaps you can short circuit your traumas and live a liberated life without having to feel it all. However, with such techniques, you still must confront it directly, then get past it.

Furthermore, what you focus on tends to grow, so by wallowing in your pain you could be making it worse. Perhaps, just getting out and living life, creating art, exploring nature, connecting with others, getting laid and drinking margaritas will be better for you than focusing on your pain.

Decide for yourself if you want to face what hurts you head on, in order to heal it, or if you prefer to avoid it or pretend it does not exist. Consider the possibility that the only way past is through.

CHAPTER 67

Stay Present With Your Triggers

A trigger is a person or an experience that usually causes you to react automatically, unconsciously and unskillfully as a result of your unhealed traumas.

On one end of the spectrum, some folks are not easily bothered and can maintain their composure under most circumstances. On the other end, some folks are triggered frequently, even by slight disturbances.

Think about yourself. Where are you on this spectrum? Do you get triggered easily? If so, by what, and by whom? What programs are running subconsciously as a result of unhealed emotional and psychological wounds that cause you to be triggered? To uncover these answers is the real dirty work, but sometimes excavating mud can lead to hidden treasures.

Trauma generally occurs when you experience a perceived threat to your safety. Whether the danger is real or not, the event causes a shock to your psyche and nervous system. This can occur as the result of a single incident, or from a set of ongoing experiences. It can come from war, violence, physical abuse, emotional abuse or any shock that provides a perceived threat. This trauma gets stuck inside of you, both physiologically and psychologically. It becomes part of who you are on an unconscious level, and determines how you respond to life when you feel threatened or unsafe – when you get triggered.

Triggers often occur in the context of human relationships. Family and romantic relationships are particularly fertile grounds for triggers to arise.

At the moment of triggering, your conscious mind tends to check out and your instincts kick in. Because the current event triggers a memory of a previously perceived danger, survival mode sets in, and the desire to fight for your life or escape is automatic and overwhelming. Or you may become immobilized, frozen in fear. The fight, flight or freeze responses are activated. You may experience a shortness of breath, tightness in your body, heat, sweating, an accelerated heart rate, a loss of mental clarity and even panic. Common reactions are to become angry and lash out, to withdraw and isolate, or to become paralyzed – unable to act.

This often causes a breakdown in communication, misunderstanding, harsh words, hurt feelings, anger, fighting and breakups in relationships. It causes disconnection and separation between people. The root cause is a disconnection from one's self in the moment of being triggered.

Staying present with your triggers allows you to stay connected with yourself and the other in the moment when your defenses arise and you tend to lose conscious control.

It requires enormous strength and courage to stay present with your triggers, because, by their very nature, they cause you to go unconscious. The thinking mind automatically checks out as you go into survival mode, and the subconscious mind takes control. Thus, when you get triggered, you are not aware that it is happening.

You must overcome your subconscious mind's automatic instinct to fight for your life, freeze or flee, because it perceives a threat, based on past experiences. As you begin to practice this self-awareness, it could be terrifying.

However, in the context of healing emotional wounds, you must become self-aware, and understand the hurt that resides within you, rather than avoiding it through escapism, or pretending it is not there. Know that you get triggered, and what your triggers are. Then, it is vitally important to recognize the moment you get triggered and stay present when it happens, allowing you to take responsibility for how you respond.

Stay Present With Your Triggers

How do you stay present, when your instinctual reaction is to go unconscious in order to preserve your life?

First, cultivate awareness as a regular way of being. Be aware that you get triggered, be aware of what your triggers are, and begin to notice them as they arise.

Second, learn to regulate your nervous system, so you can stay calm when you are triggered. Thus, rather than checking out, you can maintain conscious awareness while confronting the situation.

Your breath is key. Stay focused on your breath. Take long, slow, deep, gentle breaths when you notice yourself getting triggered. This will help you stay present and calm. You can also remind yourself that you are safe in the moment, if you can remember to do so as your survival instincts kick in.

Notice if your heart rate accelerates, your body tightens, your breath shortens, your mind fogs up, and you want to lash out or check out.

This is part of going through it, so you can come out the other side. Practices such as meditation, yoga, chi gong and Cobra Breath can help you regulate your nervous system. Remember to have a practice. Remember to practice, practice, practice. This will be a valuable tool for all aspects of your life, including giving you the resources to stay present with your triggers when they confront you.

The crucial element here is to stay present with your triggers as they arise, one way or another. This is one of the most empowering and transformative skills you can possibly cultivate in your life. It is also one of the most difficult.

When you can stay present with your triggers, you afford yourself the opportunity to transform unconscious reactivity into conscious responsiveness, thereby overcoming your subconscious, self-limiting and self-destructive programming, and creating more satisfying, rewarding and fulfilling outcomes in your life.

OPPOSITE

This life lesson is not for everyone. Life may have handed you such severe trauma that you simply cannot stay present with your triggers. It may be unbearable, and you may lack the inner resources or support systems to be able to cope with the full weight of confronting the immensity of your wounds. If this is so, then take it easy on yourself. This life lesson is purely optional.

Furthermore, some folks spend their entire lifetimes doing healing work, yet never healing. They read books, take seminars, do the positive self-talk and manifestation practices, and spend years in therapy talking about their childhood traumas – but nothing ever changes or gets better. To endlessly focus on your wounds serves no constructive purpose. Do not do that.

However, this life lesson is something entirely different. It is about applying deliberate intention to take ownership for the unhealed parts of yourself that are unconsciously sabotaging your life, and facing them directly, thereby creating greater peace within, and greater success in every one of your endeavors and human relationships.

If you wish to transcend that which holds you back in life, if you wish to master yourself, if you wish to become superhuman, then practice staying present with your triggers.

CHAPTER 68

Regulate Your Nervous System

Where are you on the spectrum of nervous system regulation? Do you have a well-regulated nervous system? Is it completely unregulated? Or are you somewhere in between? Can you regulate your nervous system when you become stressed out?

When you get triggered and go into survival mode, it is your nervous system that gets triggered. This is why deep breathing and calming internal dialogue are helpful. They can assist you in regulating your nervous system. Practices such as meditation, yoga, chi gong, and Cobra Breath are valuable aids. They help prepare you for stressful situations. Being able to regulate your nervous system allows you to stay present with your triggers, and to respond more skillfully, thereby transforming unconscious reactivity into conscious responsiveness.

Regulating your nervous system is useful not only when you are severely triggered, but at all times. Being nervous in a job interview or on a first date are common experiences. Really, these are symptoms of the "I'm not good enough" wound being triggered. Any trigger, mild or severe, is helped by regulating your nervous system.

OPPOSITE

There is absolutely no opposite to this life lesson that will ever serve you well. Having a well-regulated nervous system is always a good idea.

CHAPTER 69

Transform Unconscious Reactivity Into Conscious Responsiveness

All externally constructed layers of self aside, at the core of your being, you are Awareness. To be that which you are is to be aware.

To shed light on the dark is to become more self-aware than you previously have been. It is to become aware of your blind spots.

You can become aware of the pain in your heart, your unhealed traumas, and how you react unconsciously when they get triggered.

You can learn to regulate your nervous system, so that you can stay present with your triggers.

This is all preparation.

The next step is where all of your magic and power lie.

You can choose to transform your unconscious reactivity into conscious responsiveness.

All day every day you are reacting and responding to the events and conditions in your life. The difference is that a reaction is automatic and unthinking. A response is with deliberate intention. Aside from emergency situations and such obvious exceptions, it is generally wise to pause and reflect, before reacting or responding to anyone or anything. Responding intentionally is likely to produce more desirable results.

Sometimes, you react unconsciously to things that do not trigger you. You have a standard response to regular occurrences, so you go on autopilot.

Triggers are a different phenomenon. Your survival instinct is threatened, and you go unconscious in an instant, so your subconscious mind can save you. Things can get messy. You might get angry, say hurtful things, or get physically violent. You may withdraw from the situation as an automatic act of self-preservation. You are likely to create separation between yourself and others.

Once you have increased your awareness by shedding light on your unhealed wounds and realizing that you get triggered, the next step is to acknowledge that you have previously gone unconscious and reacted without self-awareness. These reactions tend to be destructive rather than constructive.

Now, you can stay present with your triggers, and choose to respond with deliberate intention, by remaining conscious, rather than slipping into unconscious reactivity.

This is the great work. Learn to regulate your nervous system, so you can cultivate the capacity to stay present with your triggers. Then, you can mindfully choose to transform your destructive unconscious reactivity into constructive conscious responsiveness.

This will change your life and your relationships in magnificent ways. You will create connection, rather than separation. You will create peace, rather than chaos. You will create healing, rather than wounding. This is how you cease the perpetuation of the trauma cycle. When you can master this, you are well on your way to mastering yourself.

OPPOSITE

There is absolutely no opposite to this life lesson that will ever serve you well.

CHAPTER 70

The Best Healers

This life lesson is about emotional healing. The work of medical doctors is beyond the scope of this book. When it comes to emotional and spiritual healing, the best healers are the ones farthest along their own healing paths.

The wounded healer is a common theme. People enter the healing arts because they are seeking answers for their own troubles. Without much pain to heal within themselves, they will not be drawn to these realms.

People begin to acquire skills and techniques as they journey down their healing paths, then begin to share, teach and sell them to others. A common pitfall is to believe that you are farther along the healing or spiritual path than you really are. This is false pride, not true confidence.

Be cautious when trusting self-proclaimed masters, shamans, gurus and healers. Remember, never trust an expert. When someone promotes themselves as a wise and powerful healer, remember, never trust a thin chef or a fat personal trainer. Remember, don't tell me what you can do, show me. Trust people whose actions match their words, and who can demonstrate their ability to successfully apply the knowledge and skills they purport to possess.

Generally, the best healers are the ones who have successfully done the most healing work on themselves. The results will be evident in how they carry themselves and show up in the world.

When you take a close look, you can see if someone has really done their own inner work. They are conscious and loving, they are calm and confident, they are present and kind. They have faced themselves. They are no longer ruled unconsciously by their traumas. They are in alignment. They effortlessly express their natural and authentic selves.

> They have the evidence to prove that
> they know what it takes, and have
> successfully applied it in their own lives.

Work with healers who are farthest along their own healing paths. Progress as far as you can down your own healing path. Do not tell me how many meditation, yoga, and chi gong workshops you have taken, or certifications you possess. Show me how much meditation, yoga and chi gong you do by how you engage with life and show up in the moment. How you practice is how you play. Have a practice. Practice, practice, practice. Then, show the world by example what kind of healer you are.

Now, some folks are deceptive. They act like highly evolved, superconscious, enlightened masters and healers, while attempting to conceal their darkness from the light. You must exercise discernment – the ability to feel into a person's character, authenticity and energy – to keenly observe, and read who that person really is, in contrast to who they present themselves to be. Are they healed? Or are they hiding? Are you one of these people?

Can someone ever fully heal? Perhaps yes, perhaps no. Nonetheless, there are degrees of progress that can be made. Those who have done the most healing themselves are best equipped to serve others on their healing paths. Those who claim to be great healers, but have clearly not found peace, presence, clarity and love, are to be regarded with caution.

For now, suffice it to say that the best healers are the ones who are farthest along their own healing paths.

> If you want to be a healer,
> first do the work on yourself.

The more you heal yourself, the stronger your powers will be, and the greater service you can be to others.

OPPOSITE

Perhaps a completely unconscious person who has done no healing work on themselves can be the catalyst for your own transformation and healing, by really pissing you off.

Furthermore, there are powerful healers who have not fully healed themselves, yet are still of great service to others, while continuing to grapple with their own darkness.

Yet, as a general rule of thumb, this life lesson stands firm. It will serve you well to remember that the best healers are the ones farthest along their own healing paths. This holds true for you as well.

PART TEN

Other People

CHAPTER 71

The Primary Importance Of Connection

What is important in life?

Your life's priorities will change over time, and differ from those of other people. You get to decide for yourself what is important to you.

However, there are some values shared by most, if not all humans. Most folks consider basic survival needs such as food, water, shelter, warmth and safety to be highly important, whether they know it or not.

Another common, if not universal human need is for meaningful, authentic connection with other people. This cannot be overstated. Connection is one of the greatest human needs, after the needs for physical safety and well-being.

This basic human need is well documented. A 75-year study at Harvard University discovered that the happiest people are the ones with the deepest bonds of friendship and love. In his TED talk, Johann Hari concluded that "The opposite of addiction is not sobriety. The opposite of addiction is connection." Hari presents evidence to support his thesis that addiction results from a person's lack of connection with others.

Simply put, when you have meaningful connections with other people, you are more likely to feel happy, satisfied, enriched and fulfilled. When these connections are missing from your life, you are not getting what you require to be a fully realized human being.

Think about the people in your life. Do you have meaningful, intimate and fulfilling connections with other people? Does this life lesson ring true for you?

Some folks are more introverted or extroverted. Some folks are shy or truly enjoy a solitary life. Others are gregarious and outgoing, feeling comfortable talking with everyone. Whether you are more outgoing or more reclusive, you probably thrive off of genuine human connection, at least some of the time.

On the path of self-awareness, it is wise to know your style of relating to other people. Are you an introvert or an extrovert? Is it situational? What is your level of social anxiety, or social comfort? Do you enjoy having a few close friends, or knowing everyone in town?

Regardless of your relational style and level of comfort engaging with others, make sure to cultivate meaningful, authentic connections in your life, at least with a few people.

Connection is of primary importance.

OPPOSITE

Perhaps you are in the extreme minority who prefers to live alone in a cabin in the woods. If so, go for it. Most people will be happier and more fulfilled when their need for human connection is satisfied.

Therefore, as a general rule of thumb, there is no opposite to this life lesson that will serve you well.

One caution is to be careful who you connect with. Avoid toxic, negative, pessimistic, manipulative, whiny, complaining, small minded people. Surround yourself with the right people. Be sure to have at least some meaningful, authentic and loving relationships in your life with kind, caring, positive, uplifting and supportive people.

CHAPTER 72

Every Act Creates Connection Or Separation

Connection is universally one of the most important human needs. In relation to other people, everything you do creates either connection or separation.

Every word, every act, brings you closer to other people, or farther apart. Even the simple difference between a smile or a scowl can be the difference between connection or separation.

Are you genuinely interested in other people? Do you ask meaningful questions? Do you listen attentively? Do you acknowledge and validate other people? Do you support, encourage, inspire and uplift other people? These behaviors foster connection.

Are you scared of social interactions? Do you ignore other people, not even taking notice of them? Are you ambivalent towards others? Or do you act hurtfully towards others? Do you judge, criticize and belittle people? Are you scornful, discouraging, disparaging and negative? These types of behaviors cause separation between people.

In personal and intimate relationships, accepting someone as they are versus requiring them to be who you want them to be can make the difference between creating connection or separation.

Arguments are a great way to create separation. When two people argue, they become unable to hear the other person's point of view, while insisting upon advancing their own. Neither person feels seen nor heard, and the argument can escalate into misunderstandings, hurt feelings, hurtful words spoken and broken relationships.

What if each person gave the other a chance to speak, and was willing to listen and consider what the other person had to say? This would create connection.

Consider in your own life how you relate to other people. Do you feel connected or separate? Do you act in ways that foster connection or create separation? Probably some of each.

Consider the words you speak to and about other people. Every angry, judgmental, hurtful word you speak, directly to someone or indirectly about them, serves to create more distance between the two of you.

Every kind word spoken, even indirectly, brings you closer together, thereby fulfilling one of your greatest needs and desires – connection.

Consider that even your thoughts and feelings about a person can serve to create closeness or distance, by adding a few drops of energy to the unseen cosmic fabric of all creation.

Thus, it is wise to be mindful of your thoughts, feelings, words and actions in the context of how you are always creating connection or separation between yourself and other people with what you think, how you feel, what you say, and what you do.

Human connection is one of the most important aspects of life for most people, whether they know it or not. Everything you do in relation to others creates further connection or separation. Being aware of this, you can be mindful of how you interact with other people, so as to do so in a manner that fosters connection, thereby enjoying a greater quality of life.

OPPOSITE

While it is theoretically possible that some acts may be neutral, rather than creating greater connection or separation, as a general rule of thumb, everything registers. Everything has impact. The energies you put out, no matter how small or subtle, are always adding to the overall energetic dynamic between you and other people. In this sense, everything you do creates connection or separation.

Thus, for practical purposes, there is no opposite to this life lesson that will serve you well. Think thoughts, speak words, and take actions that cultivate connection – or separation – the choice is yours.

CHAPTER 73

Find Your Tribe

Aside from the occasional reclusive hermit living alone in the woods, humans are social creatures.

People are pack animals. A sense of belonging is high on the list of human needs. People thrive when they are members of communities. There may be exceptions, people who truly enjoy being alone. Certainly, spending time alone is a good idea, so you can connect with yourself, and stay centered and grounded in the truth of who you are. Yet, in general, people need each other. Community is of great importance.

People may find community in their families, at church, with co-workers, at the pub, at the gym, in street gangs, sports leagues, community service organizations, common interest groups, or with friends who gather together for barbecues or canoeing down the river.

Consider the communities of which you are a part. Do you participate in multiple communities, only one, or none at all?

Do you enjoy having meaningful connections and shared activities and purposes? Do you feel a sense of belonging? Are you fulfilled in your community engagement?

Would you like more community?

In what types of communities might you wish to participate. Perhaps you may wish to start your own. No matter what you enjoy about life, there are others who share your interests.

Find people you can connect with on a meaningful level, one of substance, and share parts of life together.

You can be a member of multiple communities, or dedicate all of your time to a single one. If your tribe does not exist, or you cannot find it, then create your own. Either way, find people that you want to be surrounded by, interact with, and share common interests and endeavors with. It is vitally important for your emotional and psychological well-being to have community.

Perhaps this need of yours is already met. If not, then find your tribe.

OPPOSITE

Some people truly are loners. They prefer to be by themselves, or to enjoy one-on-one interactions over group encounters. They do not want to participate in community. If you are one of these people, that is fine. This life lesson is not for you.

At other times, even if you are an outgoing person who loves to participate in groups, you will certainly benefit from some alone time, stillness and silence.

However, as a general rule of thumb, most people will benefit from having and participating in community, at least some of the time. Unless you truly enjoy a reclusive life, find your tribe, or create one.

CHAPTER 74

Know, Like And Trust

This life lesson is from day one of any proper sales training. People prefer doing business with others whom they know, like and trust.

You can expand this rule of thumb to all areas of life.

People form friendships, community, intimacy, romance and partnership with other people whom they know, like and trust.

Consider the people closest to you in your personal and professional lives. They are most likely people whom you know, like and trust.

Consider yourself. When people get to know you, do they like you and trust you? How likeable and trustworthy are you?

Not everyone will like you, and you will not like everyone else. Some people are just different than you. They have discordant energies, they are on different vibrational frequencies. And that is fine. However, most people turn out to be fairly likeable, if you give them a chance. Even you.

How likeable are you? Be honest with yourself. Perhaps you are more likeable than you think. Or perhaps you are a jerk, but do not know it.

A different but related question is, how trustworthy are you?

Are you willing to lie, cheat and steal if it furthers your best interests? Or are you upfront with your transactions? Can people count on you to keep secrets and deliver on your promises?

If human connection is of primary importance, every act creates connection or separation, and people form bonds with others whom they know, like and trust, then it is advisable to allow people to get to know you, be genuinely likeable and trustworthy, and get to know others whom you like and trust as well.

Now, being likeable does not mean deviating from your true nature in order to please other people. It means to develop a sound character, which will automatically make you likeable, at least to some folks.

What does it mean to develop a sound character? The lessons in this book aim in that direction, so keep reading. Be present. Take care of yourself. Be kind. Care about other people. Keep your agreements. Be trustworthy.

Get to know people, seek to discern who is likeable and trustworthy, and align yourself with those people. Be that which you wish to see in the world as well. Be someone who others can get to know, like and trust.

OPPOSITE

There is absolutely no opposite to this life lesson that will ever serve you well. Get to know people. Allow people to get to know you. Be likeable without sacrificing your authenticity. Develop a trustworthy character.

CHAPTER 75

Belly To Belly

What is the best way to get to know someone, and for them to get to know you?

Get belly to belly with them.

That is, be in person, face to face, directly engaging with people. Meeting people in person is completely different than over the internet. You get to look into each other's eyes. You can shake hands or hug. You will reside inside each other's energy fields, which extend beyond your physical bodies. You have the opportunity to feel the other person.

Belly to belly is the best way to get to know people, build bonds, friendships and relationships of all kinds.

This is how you will get to know the people whom you like and trust. This is how you find your tribe.

Not everyone is for you, and you are not for everyone. However, if you are in alignment with yourself, live with integrity, and seek to foster connection rather than separation, you will, for the most part, get along with other people, and find those with whom you resonate.

The more you get belly to belly with other people, the more sales you will make, the more business opportunities you will encounter, the more likely you are to make friends and find romance. The more you will learn from the life experiences of others, the more opportunities for adventure will present themselves, the more fulfilling connections you will enjoy.

Take time to yourself when you need to, AND be sure to get belly to belly with others. Connecting with people over the internet does not fulfill your need for connection. Getting drunk at the pub with strangers does not truly fulfill this need. Getting belly to belly with people, getting to know them, being likeable and trustworthy, finding others who are likeable and trustworthy as well, forming bonds, and sharing meaningful conversations and experiences together does fulfill this need.

The doors of your life will swing wide open when you get belly to belly.

OPPOSITE

If you do not like other people, then stay home.

If you have extreme social anxiety or severe low self-esteem, the practice of getting belly to belly with other people may take you so far outside your comfort zone that it causes an inordinate amount of stress on your nervous system. In this case, practice expanding beyond your comfort zone slowly and gently. Get belly to belly with people just a little bit at a time.

However, for the majority of humanity, as a general rule of thumb, there is no opposite to this life lesson that will serve you well. The best way to get to know people is to get belly to belly with them, thereby fulfilling your basic human need for meaningful, authentic connection.

CHAPTER 76

Treat Everyone With Humanness

Everyone has challenges in life. Everyone has a backstory. They have difficulties, struggles, grief, loss, fears, doubts and insecurities. Just like you. They most likely have an inner life as deep and complex as yours. They have pain in their hearts, which may cause them to act hurtfully towards others. Just like you. They sometimes behave unconsciously. Just like you. Yet, most people are inherently decent human beings. Just like you.

People want their basic survival needs met. They want to feel safe and secure. They want connection and validation. They want to be seen and heard. They want to be treated with dignity and respect. They want love, sex and money. Just like you.

People want to be treated with humanness. Just like you.

Have you ever encountered someone who you could just feel was completely accepting of everyone else, exactly as they are? They were genuinely interested and caring, without the need for others to conform to their requirements or expectations.

The opposite is to compare, judge, criticize, scorn or reject another. This creates separation, and generally serves only to make you feel better than them, which is a cover for not feeling good enough.

Instead, practice treating everyone you encounter today with humanness.

Ram Dass famously said "We are all just walking each other home." This alludes to recognizing the humanness of all people. Realize that everyone is mostly the same. Everyone has challenges, suffering and pain. Everyone wants to feel peace, happiness, safety and connection. So cut people some slack. Grant others a wide berth. Allow people to be who they are. Be understanding. Be kind. Allow people to be imperfect. Give them space to breathe and to exist freely.

Ask yourself how you are with other people. Do you cut them some slack? Are you warm, accepting and welcoming? Or are you cold, judgmental and unforgiving?

Consider what life may be like when you treat everyone with humanness. Connection awaits you upon every encounter. By being an ally to others, you will be surrounded by allies. You will find an abundance of enriching connections in your life when you treat everyone kindly, even if you do not know their specific backstory.

Give people the gift of being seen and heard, and accepted just as they are. This is the true embodiment of awareness and compassion. This is advanced spirituality.

Remember to walk other people home today, and perhaps every day, for the rest of your life. Treat everyone with humanness.

OPPOSITE

Sometimes, people behave terribly. If someone is being a truly horrible person, perhaps you must meet them with decisive brutality. With situational awareness and discernment, you will have to decide. However, as a general rule of thumb, it will serve you well in life to remember to treat people with humanness.

CHAPTER 77

Don't Be An Asshole

Carl is a school teacher who spends the first day of each new school year discussing the rules of his classroom with his students. He only has one rule: Don't be an asshole.

He rarely has any disciplinary problems for the rest of the school year. His students understand that they are expected to behave respectfully, and that disrespectful behavior will not be tolerated.

To be an asshole is to behave disrespectfully.

When you are disrespectful towards others, it creates separation. You may find yourself lonely, with enemies rather than friends, and burdened by unnecessary challenges in your life.

When you treat other people with kindness, dignity and respect, you create connection. People will want to get to know you. They will like you and trust you, and they will generally respect you in return.

Now, some folks are just jerks. They will not reciprocate your respectful treatment of them. This is why you must learn to practice discernment of other people's characters. However, for the most part, people will recognize the quality of your character when you treat them with dignity and respect. Those who treat you similarly are the ones you want to keep close to you.

One specific application of this life lesson is that, when people unconsciously take out their unhealed wounds on other people, they can be real assholes. Thus, in order to not be an asshole, you can shed light on what is dark by becoming aware of your blind spots, that is, acknowledging the pain in your heart, your unhealed traumas, and know that they get triggered. Then learn to regulate your nervous system so that you can stay present with your triggers, and deliberately transform unconscious reactivity into conscious responsiveness, thereby becoming less of an asshole.

Another way to not be an asshole is to actually care about the well-being of other people, and to be genuinely interested in them. Ask them questions about themselves, listen attentively, seek to understand them, be empathetic, supportive and encouraging.

This lesson can be applied to all areas of your life. Are you being an asshole, or are you being kind, caring and respectful?

You will enjoy more connection and friendship in life when you are not an asshole. This is part of having a likeable and trustworthy character.

Quite simply, don't be an asshole.

OPPOSITE

Perhaps there are times when you need to be an asshole. Is someone behaving abusively? Is someone attempting to take unfair advantage of you? Is someone physically threatening you, filing an unjust lawsuit against you, or otherwise behaving in a hostile manner towards you without provocation. In such instances you may need to be an asshole.

However, as a general rule of thumb, it will serve you well to treat other people with kindness, dignity and respect, until it becomes situationally appropriate to do otherwise.

CHAPTER 78

Never Speak Poorly Of Others

It is generally safe to talk about someone behind their back, if what you say about them is kind, true and appropriate for the public record.

It is generally unwise to speak poorly of others, to say things that are false, or to expose private or confidential information.

Remember, every act, in relation to another, creates greater connection or further separation. Speaking poorly of other people only creates separation. It also reflects poorly upon you.

Have you ever been around someone who speaks negatively of others? They are not fun to be around. They are not likeable people. They are not building trust by speaking poorly of others. And neither are you.

Speaking poorly of other people is low-class. It makes people around you feel bad, and is a sign that you are neither likeable nor trustworthy. Others will not want to get to know you. They will want to avoid you, perhaps not even knowing why.

People are psychic on a subtle level. It could be that when you speak poorly of someone, even if they are not present, their higher self or subconscious mind can feel the unseen energetic separation you have created by talking negatively about them behind their backs.

Even worse is when they hear about it afterwards. It makes for an awkward situation. When someone hears through the grapevine that you were talking bad about them, they discover that you are neither likeable nor trustworthy, and you have lost a friend and ally, forever.

Speaking poorly of others is not classy. It is not professional. It demonstrates lack of trustworthiness. It is generally not wise to do.

Other people can feel your negativity, and no one likes it.

Simply put, speaking poorly of other people lacks integrity.

Part of having integrity, part of being likeable and trustworthy, part of creating connection rather than separation, is to never speak poorly of other people.

OPPOSITE

This life lesson definitely has exceptions. A Buddhist teaching on Wise Speech suggests to not speak poorly of other people, unless it is true, timely and necessary. Then, you must speak up. For instance, if you have a friend who is about to enter into a business deal or romantic relationship with someone who has a proven track record of being unscrupulous, then it is wise and highly advisable to warn your friend before they enter into that relationship. In such a hypothetical situation, it is true, timely and necessary to speak poorly of another person.

Otherwise, say something nice about the person, or say nothing at all. Do not participate in negative gossip, and be wary of others who do.

As a general rule of thumb, if you wish to have a dignified character, do not speak poorly of others.

CHAPTER 79

No One Likes To Be Criticized

Getting along with other people is one of the most important life skills you can master.

Get belly to belly with people. Get to know them. Allow them to get to know you. Develop a trustworthy character. Give people the experience of being seen and heard. Treat people with humanness. Don't be an asshole. Do not speak poorly of others.

Do not criticize other people. No one likes to be criticized. No one likes to have their faults pointed out.

No one likes to receive unsolicited advice.
No one likes to hear you badmouth other people.
No one likes to be criticized.

Often a person will attempt to "help" another person by offering unsolicited advice, by shedding light on their blind spots by pointing out their character flaws or inappropriate behavior. No one wants to hear it. They will put up their walls of protection and separation, and not receive the criticism constructively.

Allow people to be who they are, rather than criticizing them. You can certainly notice their behavior and their character, and navigate your course through life accordingly. However, criticism rarely helps.

If someone is behaving inappropriately, you will have greater success by modeling appropriate behavior rather than by directly confronting them.

In some instances, you may come across people who are just intolerable. It is okay to avoid them. You can practice compassion from a distance and just get away from them.

You are not likely to ever make friends by criticizing other people. It is a turn off to others when you criticize them directly, or when you criticize someone else who is absent. Even if they are not consciously aware of the reason they do not enjoy your presence, they will feel bad around you.

No one likes to be criticized. No one likes to be around people who criticize others. It creates separation, makes people feel bad, and reflects poorly on your character when you do so. Therefore, do not criticize other people.

OPPOSITE

It is wise to notice when someone is behaving inappropriately. For instance, if they are dishonest, abusive, dangerous, destructive or of low moral character. However, this is not the same as criticizing them. This is observing their character.

Therefore, there is no opposite to this life lesson that will serve you well.

As a general rule of thumb, do not criticize other people, because no one likes to be criticized.

CHAPTER 80

You Cannot Change Other People

Have you ever tried to change another person? How did that work out for you? Probably not so well.

You cannot change other people.

You have a slightly better chance of changing yourself.

Do not expect people to change. They will not.

For the most part, people are who they are.

A person's core essence does not change over time. Their outer layers might change a little. Perhaps they may become calmer and wiser as they age. Or having children will change them a little. Or they may develop greater awareness and a kinder heart. Or life might make them more cold and bitter. So yes, sometimes people change a little bit. But usually, not by much. And they never change because you tried to change them.

Plant this notion firmly in your head.

People are who they are.

They generally do not change by much, if at all. If they do change, it is for themselves, not for you.

This realization will help you throughout life, as you encounter all sorts of different people. You will find the ones with whom you resonate. You may find your tribe, close friends, business associates and romantic partners. You may find people about whom you feel neutral, and people with whom you are discordant.

When you can learn to observe a person, discern their character, and understand that people do not change, you may live with more grace and ease by aligning yourself with resonant beings, and leaving others alone. By paying attention, and using discernment, you will not have to force it. People will come and go in your life; the right ones will stay.

You can accept people as they are, because you know you cannot change them. You can practice compassion from a distance for those who are intolerable. You will flow more easily with life and with people when you learn to accept that you cannot change other people.

OPPOSITE

First, if someone sincerely wants to change themselves, you can support and encourage them in doing so.

Second, if someone is behaving severely inappropriately, you might need to confront them directly about it.

However, as a general rule of thumb, there is no opposite to this life lesson. It will serve you well in your life to remember, you cannot change other people.

CHAPTER 81

Allow People To Be Exactly As They Are

One of the greatest gifts you can give to another person is to allow them to be exactly as they are.

One of the cruelest abuses to another person is to prohibit them from expressing their true nature, scorn them for doing so, or require them to be anything other than what they truly are.

Allowing someone to be and express their true nature is to treat them with kindness, dignity and respect. It is to treat them with humanness. It creates connection.

Without judgment, criticism, rejection or scorn, with presence, compassion and acceptance, can you truly see and hear another person? Can you give them space to be that which they are?

Approval and validation are natural human needs. A feeling of being worthy, of being good enough, can cause a person to thrive. A feeling of not being good enough can do the exact opposite, it can brutally suppress the latent potential within a human being.

There are constant pressures in this world, including from parents, authority figures, peers, marketing campaigns, media and society in general, for people to behave in certain ways, and conform to social norms.

You can provide relief from these pressures, to yourself and to others, by allowing other people to be exactly as they are, and allowing yourself to be exactly as you are.

This is not to say that it is futile to change yourself. Seek to improve yourself, always keep learning, master something, become more self-aware, take one step closer to your ideal self every day, if you so choose.

Yet, everything you do not change about yourself, you must accept as it is, if you want to feel peace. You must also accept everything about other people exactly as it is, because you cannot change them, and they are not likely to change themselves.

This will serve you especially well in romantic partnerships.

If you want to do an experiment, attempt to change your partner. Notice whether this creates connection or separation. Notice if your relationship becomes more enriched and fulfilling, or less so. Notice if your partner actually changes.

You can also do the opposite experiment: Accept your partner just as they are, imperfections and all. Then, notice if a deepening of connection, intimacy and love arises.

Imagine doing the same experiment with your children. If you continually suppress them, refusing to allow them to express their true natures, and constantly demand that they be something other than that which they are, what do you think the results will be?

Or, you can accept your children as they are, and allow them to express their true nature in a supportive and nurturing environment. What do you think the results will be?

Cause and effect are always at play. All causes have effects, all effects have causes. While there are numerous, if not infinite, causal factors for any given outcome, and it may be impossible to precisely determine all the effects of any single cause you have set in motion, you can certainly use common sense and critical thinking to consider which ways of treating people are likely to lead to which types of results.

Do you want a happy and fulfilling romantic partnership, characterized by acceptance, trust and intimacy? Do you want empowered and confident children who grow up into well-adjusted and successful adults? Do you want to enjoy connection with all those you encounter?

> Consider allowing your partner,
> your children and all people
> to be exactly as they are.

If you want connection in your life, if you want fulfilling interpersonal relationships, if you want people to get to know, like and trust you, if you want to give one of the greatest gifts you can give, then allow people to be exactly as they are.

OPPOSITE

It may be that human nature is inherently neither good nor bad. It appears to be all encompassing. Sometimes people behave in hurtful ways. They can be violent, abusive, cruel and harmful. Perhaps it is wise not to tolerate such behaviors.

Aside from such instances, as a general rule of thumb, it is a good idea to accept people exactly as they are. It may be a pleasant respite from the pressure to conform to social norms. It may be a soothing antidote to the inner doubt that so many people carry of "I'm not good enough". It will make you likeable and trustworthy. It will create connection, rather than separation. It is one of the greatest gifts you can give to another person.

Aside from egregious and abhorrent behaviors, allow people to be exactly as they are.

CHAPTER 82

Practice Compassion From A Distance

In general, it is a wise practice to allow people to be exactly as they are. This fosters connection and friendship, people will feel good around you, they will want to get to know you, and they will like you and trust you. However, this does not mean you must tolerate poor behavior.

People can be pessimistic, whiny, critical, mean, disrespectful, cruel or abusive. They may demonstrate any number of behaviors that you would prefer to avoid. Or perhaps they simply have discordant vibrational frequencies to yours.

When people exhibit poor behavior, or do not resonate with you, it is perfectly reasonable to remove yourself from their proximity. You cannot change them, and they are not likely to ever change themselves. People pretty much just are who they are. You are well within your right to distance yourself from such people.

This could even be a family member, partner or friend. The cycles of family trauma and abuse tend to perpetuate themselves. People unconsciously take out their unhealed wounds onto others, especially the ones closest to them. You do not have to tolerate this. It can be sad to cut people close to you out of your life. But sometimes you need to have the dignity and self-respect to distance yourself from people who are toxic and treat you abusively, no matter who they are.

You can pray for such difficult people. You can earnestly wish them well in your heart. You can hope for them to become more self-aware, kind and loving. And you can get as far away from them as you possibly can, to preserve your own peace and sanity. You will be happier and more peaceful when you learn to practice compassion from a distance.

You have every right to disallow people from your life who treat you poorly. They may be unaware of their abusive behavior. They may even believe they are your friend and ally. However, when you can clearly observe a person's behavior and character, you are justified in avoiding those who treat you without dignity or respect, even if they do so unconsciously.

Sometimes, you need to practice compassion from a distance. Become skilled at doing so, and it will invite more grace, ease and peacefulness into your life. Then, you will find yourself surrounded by the right people.

OPPOSITE

There is no opposite to this life lesson that will serve you well. Do not tolerate poor behavior. Distance yourself from toxic people, yet, practice compassion for them from far, far away.

CHAPTER 83

Personality Versus Character

Learn to distinguish between personality and character.

Personality is your outward facing self-expression. It is your social interface with the world. For example, it may be loud, outgoing, humorous, friendly, quiet, reserved or serious.

Character is the true nature of your inner being. It is how you treat other people. It is your moral compass. It is your behaviors and habits. It is the level of your integrity.

> Personality is when you help someone,
> then post about it on social media.
> Character is how you treat that same
> person when no one is watching.

The life lessons in this book are about developing your own character, and being able to discern the character of others.

Personality is not necessarily a bad thing, however, sometimes it can be inauthentic. Your character is always the truth of who you are. Therefore, it is wise to cultivate the ability to differentiate between the outward show of who a person is, versus the true nature of their being.

Some folks have personalities well aligned with their characters. What you see is what you get. Others express personalities very different from their characters, perhaps even misleading.

A classic example of personality misrepresenting character is a skilled but unethical salesperson. They are fun and charismatic, and act like they care about you. But it is all a show. They just want your money, even if what they are selling does not benefit you.

Other folks have a high degree of alignment. Their personality is an authentic outward expression of their inner character.

Think about your close friends, business associates and romantic partners. Think about the people you know, like and trust. It is probably a combination of their characters and their personalities that attracts you. However, it is the quality of their characters that you truly admire.

The point here is to understand the difference between personality and character. These two aspects of a person can be quite different or quite aligned. When you pay close attention to people's behaviors, and exercise discernment, you may be able to notice the similarity or difference between their personality and character.

Become aware of the difference within yourself as well. Imagine if there were no difference between the two. This is what it means to be in alignment, to be that which you are. Do not be too hard on yourself if you sometimes fall short of this ideal. It is okay. You are human. But be aware.

OPPOSITE

There is no exact opposite to this lesson. Only that some people's personalities are a clear representation of their character, while other people's personalities may obscure the true nature of their character.

As a general rule of thumb, it will always serve you well to learn to distinguish between personality versus character, in yourself and in others.

CHAPTER 84

Judgment Versus Observation: It Is Okay To Measure A Man

No one likes to be judged.

Judging other people creates separation, rather than connection.

People want to be accepted as they are, without judgment, and allowed to be themselves. So do you.

Usually, when you judge someone else, they are your mirror – you are judging an aspect of yourself that you see reflected in them. Or you feel insecure about yourself, so you judge them so you can feel superior.

However, to measure a person is different than to judge them.

There is a fine line between the two, and it may be difficult to observe someone without judging them. Yet, see if you can do it. Understand that people are imperfect, and everyone is struggling with something. Grant everyone a wide berth. Yet, observe their character.

You can observe if someone's actions match their words. Do they do what they say they will do? Do they keep their agreements? Do they tell you what they can do, or show you? Do they speak poorly of others? Are they negative, complaining, criticizing and discouraging? Or are they positive, supportive, appreciative, validating and uplifting? Does their personality match their character, or hide it? What is the quality of their character? Are they likeable? Are they trustworthy? How do they treat other people? Are they purely self-serving, or do they care about others? Are they conscious? Are they aware of themselves? Are they aware of you? Are they authentic or phony? Are they unconsciously ruled by the pain in their hearts which they take out on other people? Are they abusive? Are they kind and compassionate? Do they talk <u>with</u> you or <u>at</u> you? Do they talk only about themselves, or do they ask about you, then listen?

Definitely ask the same questions of yourself. But that is not the point of this life lesson. You get the point.

While it is a valuable interpersonal skill to accept people as they are without judgment, it is an equally valuable skill to pay close attention to the quality of a person's character. You have every right to distance yourself from toxic people and those of questionable character. You may wish to practice compassion from a distance for such folks. At the very least, stay away from them.

Remember the difference between observation versus judgment. While judgment serves no constructive purpose, and only serves to create separation, it is okay to measure a man.

OPPOSITE

There is no opposite to this life lesson that will serve you well. Observing other people's characters is always a good idea.

CHAPTER 85

Be Upfront With Your Transactions

Live with integrity.

Be fair and honest.

Do not cheat other people.

If you make an agreement, keep it.

Do what you say you are going to do, when you say you are going to do it.

When you are not upfront with your transactions, word gets around. Folks will not trust or respect you. If you have a conscience, you may start to lose respect for yourself.

There is the story of a building contractor who had to move towns every few years, when his dishonesty and low-quality workmanship began to catch up to him. Eventually, enough people in town knew his name and his reputation that he could no longer find new customers. He was not upfront with his transactions.

There is another story of a building contractor who never had to bid low to win contracts, because he was always upfront with his clients. He did what he said he was going to do, for the price he had given, in the time frame he had specified. When unforeseen circumstances arose, he addressed them immediately and honestly. He did quality work, and always took his client's best interests to heart.

His clients referred him to their friends and neighbors. He always had work, even in difficult economic times. He never had to advertise, let alone flee town ahead of his unethical business practices coming to light.

When you keep your agreements, treat others with dignity and respect, and live with integrity, you will have a high level of self-respect. You will also be respected by others in return.

> People will want to get to know you.
> They will like you and trust you.

You will enjoy enriching and fulfilling relationships. The effects will snowball, that is, the positive outcomes will multiply upon themselves.

This applies to personal, community, business and intimate relationships. Although this book is not specifically about how to have successful romantic relationships, many of these life lessons are applicable, including this one. Be upfront with your transactions in romance. Seek to have a partner or partners who are upfront with their transactions as well.

This is actually where the juiciness of intimacy lies, when you and your partner can be honest and authentic, especially with sensitive subjects and matters of the heart.

If you go to a dating website, you will find people who lie about their age, or pretend they do not have emotional problems. How is that going to serve them in romance if they start off by lying to prospective partners, pretending to be something they are not? Most likely, it is not going to work out very well for these folks.

When you are upfront with your transactions, you have nothing to hide. You can just be your authentic self. You will make friends, rather than enemies. You will enjoy connection rather than separation. You will be liked and trusted. You will embody integrity. You will build confidence within yourself, and cultivate the confidence that others have in you.

You will develop a reputation. In fact, you are always developing a reputation. Therefore, the question is, what type of reputation do you wish to create?

In business, in romance, with friends and with strangers: Be upfront with your transactions.

You can also learn to observe other people, and seek to find those who will be upfront with you as well.

OPPOSITE

Are there times when it may be wise to not be upfront with your transactions? You decide for yourself on this one.

As a general rule of thumb, it will serve you well to be upfront with your transactions. Live a life built on integrity, honesty and authenticity. Develop within yourself the ability to have the difficult conversations. You will find that it actually makes life easier. This is true freedom, to be upfront with your transactions.

CHAPTER 86

Negotiation Versus Collaboration

There are two different approaches you can use when transacting with other people. You can negotiate against them, or you can collaborate with them.

One approach to engaging with other people is to hide information you know, represent false information, and seek to gain advantage over them for your own personal gain. Some folks believe that negotiation is an important skill to possess in business, romance and other relationships.

Fundamentally, negotiation requires you to not be upfront with your transactions. By its very nature, negotiation encourages dishonesty. In a negotiation, you are seeking to get as much as you can for yourself, while giving as little as possible to the other party. Your goal is to maximize your own gain, regardless of whether there is benefit or detriment to the other. This may induce you to keep secrets and misrepresent yourself, in order to win the upper hand. This type of behavior certainly does not foster connection, and inherently lacks integrity.

A more enlightened perspective on negotiation is that both parties will exchange value, and will be better off. In this sense, negotiation borders with collaboration. Yet, there will always be an element of trickery, dishonesty, manipulation and mistrust in negotiation, by its very nature.

In some situations, a wiser approach than negotiation is collaboration.

Imagine being open, honest and upfront with your transactions. Consider seeking agreements that are as optimal as possible for everyone involved. Collaborating with other people, you are not looking to gain advantage over them, as in negotiation. You work together for mutual benefit. There is no need to hide anything. In sharing there is strength.

In modern society it is acceptable to benefit at the expense of another. This is often how profits are made. This is how you succeed in negotiation.

In communities where people depend on each other, folks do not behave this way. They do not negotiate, seeking to benefit at the expense of their neighbors. Rather, they collaborate for the benefit of all.

A common belief is that survival of the fittest is a natural law. Those who can out-compete others are the evolutionary winners. However, there is evidence to suggest that the best way to survive and to thrive is to work together with other people, rather than competing against them.

Consider then, do you stand to gain more when you compete against other people, or when you work together for mutual benefit? Where in your life do you negotiate, and where do you collaborate? At a car dealership, you will most likely be negotiating. On a team executing a project, you are more likely to be collaborating.

Some relationships and marriages operate by negotiation. Others, more so by collaboration. Which would you guess are the more enjoyable and fulfilling relationships and marriages? The ones based on negotiation, or collaboration?

OPPOSITE

Are there times when negotiation is better than collaboration? If an adversary is seeking to maximize their advantage over you, then perhaps you must compete against them, for example, in business situations.

Yet, in general, consider how you may wish to transact with other people. Consider that you may be more connected with others, and live a more easeful and abundant life, when you seek to work with other people, rather than against them. Understand the difference between negotiation versus collaboration.

CHAPTER 87

Trust Is Earned, Not Freely Given

Betrayal is a universal human experience. Every child eventually realizes that their parents are not 100% trustworthy.

As you go through life, strangers, friends, business associates and romantic partners will break your trust. You will also break theirs.

Broken trust can be minor, like when you agree to attend a gathering, then later change your mind, but never communicate this to the host.

Broken trust can be inadvertent, like when someone confides in you a secret, does not explicitly ask for confidentiality, and you divulge the information to others, not realizing the implied intention of privacy.

Broken trust can be intentional, like when someone charges you an unfair price for goods or services, knowing they are taking advantage of you.

Broken trust can be caused by lust. How often does one partner in a committed monogamous relationship cheat on the other?

There are infinite variations of how humans betray each other. Can you remember times when you have been betrayed? It feels horrible, right? Can you remember times when you have betrayed others? If you have a conscience, this probably feels horrible too.

The most fulfilling relationships are with people whom you trust and who trust you. It feels good to be dependable to others. It feels wonderful to have people that you know you can depend on too.

Gay Hendricks once said, "there is no such thing as a minor lapse of integrity", suggesting that integrity is all or nothing. He is a wise man, however, the truth is that even good people have lapses of integrity. Even people who are almost always trustworthy may break your trust, in a moment of weakness, need, or unconsciousness.

Eventually, you will need to trust other people. Yet, be careful when you do. Build trust gradually, rather than giving it away freely. Over time, folks will show you their true characters. They can earn your trust, and if you are trustworthy, you will earn theirs. If they are not trustworthy, time will usually tell.

Cultivate familiarity and friendship with other people. Get to know them. Observe their behaviors before giving them your trust. Do their actions match their words, or not? Are they only looking out for themselves, or do they look out for others as well? Can you confide in them? Would you give them the keys to your home when you are out of town? Would you be comfortable lending them your tools, or money? How does their energy feel? What do their behaviors say?

Consider, before placing your trust in someone, have they earned it?

Remember, trust is earned, not freely given.

OPPOSITE

Sometimes, you will need to trust strangers, such as a dentist, doctor, auto mechanic, employer or client. Sometimes, you can only learn if someone is trustworthy after you have given them your trust.

However, as a general rule of thumb, give people a chance to earn your trusts – or not – rather than giving your trust away freely.

CHAPTER 88

Trust Is Easier To Maintain Than To Repair

Over time, you can earn someone's trust, by behaving in a trustworthy manner. You can learn to trust others by observing their behaviors, and building familiarity and friendship.

Before trust is broken, there is a purity to a relationship.

Once trust is broken, it may be difficult, if not impossible, to repair. You may never be able to gain 100% confidence with that person again.

Sometimes, trust can be broken in little ways. For instance, you tell someone you will go to their party Friday night, and then you do not show up. This is a small violation of trust. Some folks do things like this all the time. If you do this, your words do not mean much. It demonstrates that your actions do not match your words, and that you are not 100% reliable.

Other times, the breaking of trust is more significant. For instance, if you are in a committed, monogamous relationship, then cheat on your partner, you will most likely never regain complete trust, and if you do, it will probably take an extraordinary effort.

Betrayal is a universal human experience.

Betrayal can be devastating to the human psyche. The absence of betrayal can be profoundly healing.

Everything you do creates connection or separation, including how you build or break trust, and whether or not you betray other people.

Imagine relating to others such that you do not betray them, even though you yourself have been betrayed in the past.

Humans are imperfect creatures, including you. You will probably not always honor your word. You may not be 100% trustworthy to all people at all times. Forgive yourself for this.

Yet, do your best to live with integrity. Keep your agreements. If you say you are going to do something, do it. Be an honorable person. Be a person of your word. Be someone whom other people can rely upon, and trust. Be someone who does not betray other people.

Build trust with other people, and maintain it through your consistent actions. Remember, it is easier to maintain unbroken trust, than to repair trust once it is broken.

OPPOSITE

There is no opposite to this life lesson that will serve you well.

It is easier to maintain trust than to repair it.

CHAPTER 89

Develop A Trustworthy Character

Be trustworthy. Be honest. Tell the truth. Do not deceive, lie, cheat or steal. Be upfront with your transactions.

Match your actions to your words. Match your personality to your character. Do not tell me what you can do, show me. Do what you say you are going to do. Keep your agreements. Be reliable. Develop and maintain a trustworthy character.

Do not speak poorly about other people unless it is true, timely and necessary. Do not be an asshole. Treat others with humanness, kindness, dignity and respect.

Have an erect posture. Hold your chin high, but not too high. Face people squarely. Look into their eyes, not intensely, but with a gentle grace. Have a firm handshake, and a warm hug.

Take care of yourself. Take care of your physical, mental, emotional, spiritual and financial health.

Be firmly and unshakably grounded in the truth of who you are. Be that which you are.

Lead and teach through your way of being in the world.

Communicate clearly and directly. Allow no bullshit in your life, ever.

Live your life in these ways, and you will develop a trustworthy character.

Your character will be evident to others. People will want to get to know you. They will feel good around you. They will like you and trust you. Your behavior will be a model for others, and you will create connection wherever you go.

It has been said that there is no such thing as a minor lapse of integrity. Either you are in integrity, or out of integrity. However, the human experience tends to be a bit more nuanced than this.

Some folks may be complete scoundrels until the day they die. Others may have a rigid morality completely unforgiving of any lapse of perfect integrity. Most folks are somewhere in between. They are fairly decent people, but may tell a lie to stay out of jail or save their mother's life, and they probably care more about themselves than they do about you.

Where are you on this spectrum of integrity? How trustworthy is your character?

The truth is, you could spend your entire life searching for a person with perfect integrity, and never find one. Yet, the people closest to you most likely have somewhat trustworthy characters, at least in relation to you.

Everything you do creates either connection or separation between you and other people. When you act out of integrity, it creates separation. When you are trustworthy, it creates connection. Human connection is universally one of the most important elements of life. By developing a trustworthy character, you will enjoy more and deeper connections, thereby satisfying one of your greatest needs.

You will have a calm, quiet confidence in yourself, knowing that you have a trustworthy character. Other people will know it too. You will not have to tell them. It will be evident in how you show up in life and move through the world.

OPPOSITE

There is absolutely no opposite to this life lesson that will ever serve you well. Develop a trustworthy character.

CHAPTER 90

The Value Of Validation

Although each human being has a unique blueprint, temperament, set of experiences, and manner of responding to life, there are some common characteristics that everyone shares.

Humans need air, water, food, sex, shelter, warmth and dryness.

Humans need to feel safe and secure.

Humans need to feel connected to others, to have a sense of belonging.

Humans need to be loved. Humans need to be touched, and to be held.

Humans need to be seen and heard. Human beings require external validation.

Aside from basic survival needs, the need for validation is one of the greatest human needs. In order to be a well-adjusted, healthy and happy person, one generally must receive sufficient levels of external validation, especially early in life. Validation is to be seen and heard, to be accepted as you are, to receive feedback from others that you are enough.

There is a modern myth that you must not seek external validation, but must love yourself completely from within. This is a grand ideal, and a worthy goal to strive after. Yet, it is also wise to acknowledge the very real human need for external validation, both in yourself and in others.

Mirroring is when a parent reflects back to a child its facial expressions, sounds, movements, behaviors and emotions. This gives the child a strong and stable sense of self. It is a form of external validation. Sufficient mirroring helps a new human being develop a well-adjusted self-awareness and ability to relate to others.

> **Without proper mirroring, a child may not develop a secure sense of self, or the ability to relate to other people in a healthy manner.**

In attachment theory, some folks are considered to have a secure attachment style, where they can relate to romantic partners with relative ease and confidence, not being too insecure or clingy. Insecure attachment styles, on the other hand, are when people become jealous and overly needy, or push their partner away in an unhealthy manner.

A secure attachment style is developed in a child's formative years, when they receive a sufficient level of attuned parenting. In other words, when the child is seen and heard – or validated – by its parents.

> **Without a sufficient level of attuned parenting, a child may not receive the external validation it requires to develop into a psychologically healthy, secure, confident human being.**

The examples of mirroring and attuned parenting demonstrate that healthy human development requires external validation.

When a young child does not receive sufficient amounts of external validation that naturally help them to develop a secure sense of self and healthy ways of relating to other people, they may spend the rest of their lives seeking external validation in unhealthy and inappropriate ways.

Now, attuned parenting comes on a spectrum, no parent is perfect. Furthermore, everyone internalizes the love they did or did not receive from their parents differently. Thus, everyone is somewhere on the spectrum of self-worth. The level of external validation they received in their early developmental stages often plays a key role in this.

You can often tell when someone has a deep and unmet need for validation. They only talk about themselves. They never ask you about yourself. They are always seeking to demonstrate their worth to others, and seeking attention and approval.

Another indication that someone has not overcome their invalidation wound is that they will often invalidate others automatically, like a reflex. They unconsciously pass on the invalidation wounds they received.

Conversely, having received sufficient external validation during the most formative years of development, a grown person may be more easily able to love themselves, find validation internally, and not seek external validation as an adult.

When someone listens attentively to you when you speak, without the need to steal the spotlight, and when they are positive and uplifting, rather than disparaging, you may consider that this person has a lesser validation wound, a lesser need to be seen and heard, and a healthier relationship with self-validation, than someone who is seeking to fill their validation void.

Nonetheless, even people who have a strong and secure sense of self enjoy being validated.

Just ask anyone in a romantic relationship where their partner ignores them, invalidates them, or treats them like shit. No one likes to be treated in an invalidating manner. Even a confident and secure person wants to be seen and heard, complimented, appreciated and loved.

So, it is a wonderful ideal to remember that you can live your life without needing external validation. This is true inner peace and self-mastery. It is pure authentic confidence. It is total trust in and acceptance of yourself. It is a beautiful state of being in which to reside, when and if you get there.

Yet, do not be surprised or disappointed if you fall short of this ideal, as promoted by the new-age spiritual gurus who sell millions of books telling you that you can be happy no matter what, and that needing external validation is a character flaw, and something to be eradicated from within yourself.

Do not believe people who tell you that external validation is not necessary. They are wrong. Everyone needs validation. What is validation? It is to be acknowledged. To be seen and heard. To be witnessed. To be allowed to be that which you are. To be told that you are good enough. To be accepted. To be loved.

Remember to validate your children, your partner and other people. Give that which you wish to receive. Yet, remember not to force it. Do not go overboard with exaggerated or phony attempts to validate other people. Validation is not about giving sugary sweet compliments or overbearing attention. It is about treating people with dignity and respect, as if they are worthy of your time and attention, worthy of love and acceptance, worthy of the oxygen they breathe, worthy of a place here on earth.

In order to validate other people, all you have to do is show up for them. Give them the gift of being seen and heard. Give them the gift of your time and true attention. These acts convey the message "you are enough". These are some of the greatest gifts in the world.

> Giving the gift of validation to others fulfills one of the most important human needs and desires: To be seen and heard.

OPPOSITE

Absolutely seek within yourself an inner knowing that you are good enough. Develop an unshakable self-reliance independent of external validation. Furthermore, be someone who gives validation, rather than seeks it. This alone is an incredibly healing and generous act.

Yet, there is no opposite to this life lesson that will serve you well. To be seen and heard is one of the greatest human needs. To not see or hear another is one of the greatest cruelties. Always remember the value of validation, and make a habit of giving it away freely and sincerely.

CHAPTER 91

Showing Up Versus Showing Off

Can you guess the difference between showing up versus showing off?

Think about it for a moment. You probably can.

When you show up for someone, you are present with them. You give them the space to speak about and express themselves. You ask them questions, then listen attentively. You are interested in who they are, and what they are feeling, thinking and doing with their life. You are acknowledging them, witnessing them, and letting them know that they are worthy of your time and attention, that they are inherently good enough. You are giving them the gift of being seen and heard, one of the greatest gifts you can possibly give to another human being.

When you are showing off, you are seeking to receive all of these same gifts from the other. You are seeking attention and validation. You are asking to be seen and heard. You talk about yourself, rather than listen to the other. You are thinking about what you are going to say while the other is speaking, rather than listening to understand. You are being interesting, rather than interested.

In a balanced relationship, both people have a chance to talk about themselves and a chance to listen. Each person will genuinely care about witnessing the other person, while also fulfilling their own need to be seen and heard by the other. There is an equal exchange of energy, both people give the gift of validation and receive it.

When you are feeling the pain, consciously or unconsciously, of your unhealed invalidation wound, your soul desires for this pain to be soothed. You long to be seen and heard. Your impulse is to have this basic human need fulfilled.

However, this can lead to a situation where you may be unconsciously demanding that people pay an inordinate amount of attention to you. This is a non-consensual exchange. This is called being an energy vampire, or giving off sticky energy: It happens when you require other people to show up for you, while you show off. This is the difference between talking <u>at</u> someone, versus talking <u>with</u> them.

Have you ever engaged with someone who only talks about themselves, and shows no interest in you? It gets old quickly, right?

Have you ever been talking about yourself, and realized that you have been hoarding the airwaves? It is a bit embarrassing, right?

When you interact with other people, do you show up, do you show off, or do you find a balance between the two?

> **When you are comfortable in your own skin, and not ruled by your invalidation wound, it is easier to show up and listen, rather than show off by talking.**

However, even if you are a well-adjusted human being with a secure sense of self, even if you received a sufficient level of mirroring, attuned parenting and external validation in your early formative years to develop a healthy style of relating to yourself and others, or even if you have overcome your invalidation wound, you probably still thrive in an environment where you are seen and heard.

Absolutely seek to find those interpersonal relationships that go both ways, where each person takes turns talking and listening, witnessing and being witnessed.

Start by being the one who listens.

OPPOSITE

If you are a performance artist, when you are on stage, it is your time to show off. When you are giving a sales, educational or informational presentation, it is your time to show off. There are times when it is appropriate to show off.

Yet, in human relationships, there is no opposite to this life lesson. It will serve you well to understand the difference between showing up versus showing off. Remember to show up for other people. Ideally, also find those who will show up for you.

CHAPTER 92

What's In It For Me?

People are self-interested. So are you.

Looking out for your own self-interest is natural, normal and healthy. Everyone does it. So do you. Everyone you encounter cares more about themselves than they do about you, and this is perfectly fine.

It will serve you well to remember this as you interact with others. Each individual sees the world through their own unique lens, from their own first-person perspective, and from their own selfish needs and desires.

Everyone wants to know "What's in it for me?"

Whether you are selling something, seeking to get a date, asking for help, talking about yourself, or anything else, remember that people are self-interested.

This is why showing up versus showing off, being interested versus interesting, and talking with versus talking at people are such valuable ways of being. Because the other person receives something valuable. You are satisfying their need to be seen and heard. That is what is in it for them.

"What's in it for me?" is one of the first lessons in sales. People do not care whether or not you earn a sales commission off of them. They care about whether or not the product or service you are selling, in exchange for the price you are asking, will benefit them.

The same is true in intimate partnerships. Each person wants to have their own needs and desires fulfilled in the relationship. Both people want to feel good, and use the other to accomplish this.

In a more expansive relationship, be it business, personal or romantic, both parties might acknowledge the "what's in it for me?" perspective, and additionally seek to collaborate, so as to serve the other. Both parties might ask "What's in it for us? How can we serve each other and satisfy our needs and desires together?"

To begin with, acknowledge and remember that, in every instance, every interaction, every transaction, every person is always interfacing with the world from this perspective:

"What's in it for me?"

OPPOSITE

Sometimes, people act altruistically. Consider, for instance, what parents may do for their children.

Yet, it can be argued that one of the greatest highs on earth is being of service to other people. Thus, even an altruistic act serves to make the person who does it feel great. Altruism literally causes the body to create feel-good chemicals. In this sense, even selfless acts are selfish.

Now, it is not necessary to pick apart other people's behaviors to determine how altruistic or selfish each act is. Simply remember that people are self-interested.

Thus, there is no opposite to this life lesson. It will always serve you well to remember that other people, consciously or subconsciously, are always asking, "What's in it for me?" And so are you.

CHAPTER 93

Communication Is Of Primary Importance

Connection is one of the greatest human needs. Connection happens through communication.

Everything you do in relation to other people creates connection or separation. This includes verbal and non-verbal communication.

Every piece of information transmitted between you and another, or lack thereof, is bringing you closer to, or further away from them. Clear, direct, honest communication, therefore, is incredibly valuable as a skill, habit and way of being. Understand the primary importance and value of communication. Learn to practice clear communication.

Some folks suggest that the masculine style of communication is more straightforward, while the feminine style of communication is less direct. This could be why men will accuse women of "playing games", and why women will find unintended hidden meaning in what men say. Each expects the other to communicate the same way as they do, but each tends to have an inherently different style of communication.

Indeed, there are differences between men and women, masculine and feminine, including styles of communication.

However, this life lesson transcends gender polarity. In general, be clear and direct in your communication. It cuts out all the bullshit, and makes life more graceful and easy.

In intimate relationships, learn to communicate your needs and desires. In fact, this can be incredibly hot and sexy. Clear communication can build intimacy, connection and trust. Think of everyone you know who are in romantic partnerships. Who has the healthiest, happiest, most successful relationships? Most likely it is the people with the best communication between partners.

With clear communication, you are being your authentic self and you are being upfront with your transactions. You are demonstrating your trustworthy character. You will find those with whom you resonate. Tell it like it is. No bullshit, ever. Be a person of your word. Straight talk is where it's at.

Now, most folks have struggles in their lives and pain in their hearts. How many people have some emotional and psychological problems? They may feel that they are not good enough. They may long to be seen and heard. They may have insecure attachment styles. They may not be straight talkers. They may not be committed to cultivating trustworthy characters or meaningful human connection. You may not be able to practice clear communication with everyone.

When you encounter people who are not straight shooters, you may wish to practice compassion from a distance. Be on guard, and maintain your boundaries. Find people who talk straight, and be such a person yourself.

> Conflict and separation often arise
> from absent, unsuccessful or hurtful
> communication. Connection arises from
> sincere, direct and effective communication.

How do you communicate? Is there an equal exchange of energy, a give and take? Or does one person hog the airwaves? Do you truly listen to what the other has to say? Can you receive communication clearly? Do you offer confirmation that you understand what has been said? Are you disparaging, invalidating and pessimistic, or kind, supportive and encouraging?

Are you able to communicate clearly when it is your turn to speak? Are you able to express yourself successfully? Are you able to see, hear and sense the ever-present nonverbal communication that is always occurring? Are you aware of it emanating from you?

Remember that communication is a two-way street. Listen more than you talk. Be interested, not interesting. Show up, rather than show off. Talk with, not at, other people. Ask questions and listen. Listen to understand, not to respond. Then speak, when necessary. Ideally, there is a mutually agreeable two-way exchange of energy and information in your relationships, where both people take turns talking and listening.

The point here is to be aware of how you communicate with other people, and to remember the primary importance of communication.

OPPOSITE

Sometimes, it is best to say nothing. Speak only when your words are true, timely and necessary, or when they are kind. Do not speak poorly of other people. Not all communication is wise communication.

For instance, there is a difference between being brutally honest and compassionately honest. Perhaps, in some instances, to be brutally honest is compassionate. If someone is self-destructive with their health, finances, relationships or life, it can be a compassionate act to be brutally honest with them about their unwise behaviors.

At other times, to be brutally honest is cruel. With situational awareness and discernment, you will know when to exercise brutal versus compassionate honesty. Usually, the latter is more wise.

As a general rule of thumb, there is no opposite to this life lesson. Communication is of primary importance, including those times when it is nonverbal, when it is best to be compassionately honest rather than brutally honest, or when it is best to say nothing at all. Always remember the primary importance of communication, in all its forms.

CHAPTER 94

Pay Attention To Non-Verbal Communication

A significant amount of communication between people is non-verbal. You communicate with others through your body language, facial expressions, eye contact, physical touch and tone of voice. Perhaps even through the ether, with your thoughts, feelings and energy.

Body language and facial expressions can convey a lot of information. How does someone carry themselves physically? Are they hunched over, or standing erect? Are they rigid or soft? When speaking together, are you facing each other directly, or facing off to the side, with only your shoulders pointing at each other? Are your arms and legs crossed, indicating that you are closed off or protecting yourself? Or are you fully open, even exposed?

A smile or a frown is non-verbal communication. You can indicate a friendliness or hostility towards others using only the muscles in your face. Have you ever noticed how people soften to you when you simply smile at them?

When you look a person in the eyes, there is an exchange of information. Some folks believe that the eyes are a window into the soul. When you look someone in their eyes, could it be that your souls are communicating non-verbally?

Consider a handshake or a hug. Is the handshake firm, or limp? Is the hug warm and sensual, or cold and rigid? How much information is exchanged through physical touch?

Consider listening to the tone in someone's voice. The same words, spoken with different intonations, can communicate very different sets of information.

Simply by paying attention to non-verbal communication, such as body language, facial expressions, eye contact, touch and tone of voice, you gain a lot of information. You may be able to notice how someone is feeling, what level of interest they have in interacting with you, how relaxed or tense they are, and so on.

There are also unseen energetic forces at play. Have you noticed that you do not choose who you are attracted to? Sometimes, you just resonate with other people, as friends or in romance. You cannot help it. This is an example of non-verbal communication. It is as if a non-physical part of your being is engaging with the non-physical part of someone else's being.

You have energy fields that emanate from, and extend beyond your physical body. Thus, by being in proximity to another person, you are residing in each other's fields, and communicating energetically. If you pay close attention, you may be able to actually feel or sense another person's energy.

> Body language, facial expressions, eye contact, physical touch, tone of voice, energy fields – there are numerous ways in which you are always communicating non-verbally with others.

Paying attention to these forms of non-verbal communication gives depth and texture to your human interactions, and you may be surprised at how much information you can gather.

You may wish to consider how you communicate non-verbally to those you encounter. What messages are you sending out all day, every day, to everyone in your vicinity?

Is your posture erect, slouched or hunched over? Does your voice waver, or is it firm? Are your hugs and handshakes firm or weak? Do you avoid eye contact, stare at people intensely, or engage in gentle eye contact? What are your eyes saying? Are you aware of your energy body? How does your energy impact those around you?

Remember to be mindful of how you are always sending out non-verbal communication. Also tune in to what others are saying without words.

OPPOSITE

There is absolutely no opposite to this life lesson that will ever serve you well.

Everyone is always sending out numerous forms of non-verbal communication. It is almost as if everyone is psychic.

Pay attention to non-verbal communication: Body language, facial expressions, eye contact, physical touch, and even people's energies. Be mindful of how you are communicating non-verbally as well.

CHAPTER 95

Pride Versus Confidence

Can you guess the difference between pride versus confidence?

Pride often comes across as confidence, but there is a difference. Pride is arrogance. It is false confidence. An arrogant person needs to tell you how great they are, because they do not truly believe it on a subconscious level, so they need you to believe it. Pride is a veil over insecurity. Pride arises out of the common human experience of the feeling "I'm not good enough, not worthy of love and acceptance".

Pride is loud. Pride is showing off. Pride is being interesting. Pride is talking at someone.

Confidence speaks for itself.

Confidence is quiet. It is an inner knowing that you are enough. When you are confident, not proud, you can show up rather than show off, be interested rather than interesting, and talk with rather than at other people.

When you are confident, your need to feel seen and heard, to be validated, is not so big as when you are proud.

When you are confident, you do not tell people what you can do, you show them. Even if you are a master of your craft, you do not need to call yourself an expert. Your work speaks for itself.

When you are confident, you do not need to tell people how great you are. The way in which you walk through the world is a sufficient expression of your worth.

As soon as you need to tell people how wonderful you are, you are no longer confident, you are proud.

The key here is to be mindful of the difference between false pride and true confidence.

Notice other people's levels of pride versus confidence. Do not be fooled by people's pride. Their true confidence will be quieter, and will speak without words.

> Pride is loud. It is showing off. Pride is a thin veil for insecurity. It covers up the fear of not being good enough. Confidence is quiet. It is knowing you are good enough. Confidence speaks with actions, pride speaks with words.

Become aware within yourself of where you stand on the spectrum of pride versus confidence. Do you have a calm, quiet, assured confidence in your inherent worthiness, or do you seek external validation, hoping to prove your worth to others, and to your doubting self? Probably some of each.

You may be surprised to discover that part of you that is longing to be seen and heard, witnessed and approved of by others. Or, it may be a familiar old friend. Or perhaps, you already know your worth, and this is not your challenge in this lifetime.

Either way, seek to notice when and if you are acting from a place of showing off and being interesting, and see if you can move, ever so gently, one small step at a time, away from insecure pride, and towards true confidence.

The life lessons in this book are practices intended to guide you on just such a journey, so that you can lay down your pride, and simply reside in the knowing that you are enough. However, reading these pages alone will not do the trick. You must implement these lessons. As you do, you will build a strong foundation of quiet confidence. Pride – underpinned by that nagging fear that you might not be good enough just as you are – will lose its power over you and fade away, supplanted by an unshakable inner knowing that "I am enough".

OPPOSITE

Pride has different connotations in different contexts. Sometimes pride is a positive attribute that is well justified. You might be proud of your child who got good grades in school or demonstrated an act of kindness towards others. You might be proud of the charitable work you do in this world. Perhaps you find pride in your creative self-expression such as music or art.

Pride is not inherently bad. Often, people do great things, and are justified in being proud of their achievements.

On the flip side of this coin, sometimes people are overly confident. Being overly confident can get you into trouble, or even killed.

Therefore, this life lesson is fluid, not rigid. Sometimes pride is good, and confidence not so much.

The point here is to be aware of the difference between false pride, which may be an expression of the feeling "I'm not good enough", and true confidence, which is the inner peace of self-validation. Understand the difference between false pride and true confidence, within yourself and in others.

CHAPTER 96

Grant Everyone A Wide Berth

A berth is a space in a harbor to park your boat.

To grant everyone a wide berth means to give everyone ample space to park their boat, to be themselves, to be imperfect, to make mistakes, to be human. It means to cut people some slack.

Everyone has their troubles, pain in their hearts, challenges in their lives. Everyone struggles with something.

Rarely is anyone 100% present and conscious at all times. Rarely does anyone love themselves 100% at all times. Rarely does anyone reside in a perpetual state of complete inner peace. Rarely is anyone always 100% honorable, trustworthy and acting with 100% integrity. Including you.

People make mistakes. People are self-interested. Sometimes they are unconscious, not self-aware, or behave without respect or integrity. Sometimes their actions do not match their words. Sometimes, people who love you will betray your trust, or invalidate you.

Give people some space to be imperfect. Give them a little bit of forgiveness.

You may witness someone acting pridefully. You may see that their pride is not true confidence, but rather an expression of their underlying feeling of not being good enough. Yet, rather than judge and scorn them, you can approach them with compassion and understanding.

It is wise to pay attention to the quality of a person's character. Notice if they are kind and caring, or insensitive and cruel. Notice if they do what they say, or if they say one thing and do another. You can notice consistent patterns of behavior, and someone's levels of awareness, compassion, trustworthiness and integrity.

However, you can also understand that nobody is perfect, and you can forgive them their minor imperfections, allowing them to simply be just as they are.

To grant people a wide berth is just this: have compassion and understanding for other people. This will always serve you well. It will create connection. It will make you likeable and trustworthy.

Cut people some slack. Grant them a wide berth.

OPPOSITE

Sometimes, people are truly assholes. You do not need to always cut people slack. If someone is behaving in a severely inappropriate manner, you are justified in confronting them about it, or distancing yourself from them. This is when you can practice having compassion from a distance, by understanding that they may simply lack the inner resources to behave appropriately, given the troubles in their lives, the disturbances in their minds and hearts.

In the extreme instances when someone is behaving terribly, you do not need to tolerate it. Aside from such times, as a general rule of thumb, grant everyone a wide berth.

CHAPTER 97

Stop Judging Other People

Judging other people is reverse sticky energy. It is the energy of repulsion.

Often, if not always, judging others is a sign that you do not approve of yourself. When you judge another, they are usually a mirror for you. There is an aspect of yourself that you see reflected in them, and you are judging that. Often, this is one of your blind spots, something you do not see about yourself, an aspect of yourself about which you are unaware, and a part of yourself that you reject.

For instance, if you are constantly judging people for being inconsiderate, there is a good chance that you are sometimes inconsiderate, possibly not aware of it, and dislike this aspect of yourself.

Or perhaps you just feel insecure, and by judging other people, you feel superior to them. This is another reason some folks judge others.

No matter what, when you judge other people, it serves no constructive purpose. It props you up with a false sense of pride. It creates separation, rather than connection. Drops of energy are being added to the infinite field of formless source energy that permeates all of creation, even when you judge other people silently to yourself.

Allowing other people to be exactly as they are creates connection, even if it is just a feeling or a thought.

When you stop judging other people, it may be a sign that you have accepted yourself as you are. This is a reflection of how you can allow yourself to be as you are, because you allow others to be as they are.

When you are at peace with yourself, when you are confident, not proud, when you can show up rather than show off, be interested rather than interesting, and talk with rather than at other people, you may be able to allow people to be as they are, forgive them their imperfectly human ways, grant them a wide berth, and stop judging them.

Have you ever encountered someone who just allows everyone to be who they are, and accepts everyone unconditionally, with compassion and understanding? It feels good to be around such people, right?

Now, imagine being such a person yourself.

This is one expression of true self-mastery: To completely allow other people to be just as they are, and to do the same for yourself as well.

Become aware of how you judge other people. Consider it a reflection of rejected or unconscious parts of yourself. Consider how you may feel like you are not good enough, and by judging other people it makes you feel like you are better than them.

Seek to allow others to be as they are, and accept them as they are, rather than judging them. This also means accepting yourself as you are, imperfections and all.

When you can master the skill of allowing people to be as they are, without judgment, you will have mastered one of the most important skills in interpersonal human relationships. You will also have mastered one of the most important skills in your relationship with yourself. It is two sides of the same coin.

Stop judging other people. And stop judging yourself.

OPPOSITE

It is okay to measure a person. This may look the same as judgment, but it is not. When you measure a person, you are determining the quality of their character and their level of trustworthiness. You may wish to avoid certain people after measuring them, perhaps practicing compassion from a distance.

However, judgment implies scorn and criticism, and pretending that you are better than someone because they are different than you. It does not serve you or other people to be judgmental.

As a general rule of thumb, there is no opposite to this life lesson that will serve you well.

Stop judging other people. And stop judging yourself.

CHAPTER 98

Stop Hurting Other People

Hurt people hurt people. Everyone has pain in their hearts, to some extent. People tend to unconsciously pass their unhealed wounds on to other people. They hurt others in the way that they have been hurt. This is what it means that hurt people hurt people.

This is the perpetuation of the cycle of trauma that has been going on since, quite possibly, the beginning of human existence. It is up to you to cease the perpetuation of the trauma cycle. The choice is yours. If you want to live your best life, contribute to the conscious evolution of humanity, heal yourself and facilitate the healing of others, love as fully as you can, experience truly fulfilling connection with others, and stop being an asshole, you absolutely MUST make this choice: Stop hurting other people.

Become aware of the pain in your heart. Heal this pain, to the extent that you can. Cultivate awareness, so that you can become aware of your triggers. Learn to regulate your nervous system, so that you can stay present with your triggers. Then, transform unconscious reactivity into conscious responsiveness, so that you no longer take your pain out onto other people. Treat other people with loving kindness, with dignity and respect. Treat other people with humanness. Give everyone a wide berth. Stop hurting other people.

OPPOSITE

There is no opposite to this life lesson that will serve you well. Make the decision to no longer pass your pain on. Stop hurting other people.

CHAPTER 99

Stop Hurting Yourself, Start Taking Care Of Yourself

Now you have come full circle. You have read through life lessons about your relationships with yourself, life, the world and other people.

You have come to the end, and now you are back to the beginning. You realize the wisdom to stop hurting other people. You are ready to stop hurting yourself. It is time to start taking care of yourself. Go back to lesson number one – take care of yourself first. No one else is going to do it for you.

Some of you folks reading this may already be taking wonderful care of your health and your life. Perhaps you eat nutritious foods, exercise regularly, have close loving relationships, joyful romance, financial abundance, fulfilling work, passionate pursuits and creative self-expression. Perhaps you have all the self-discipline in the world to take care of yourself completely at all times, with no weakness and never a lapse in will power.

Others may be just the opposite. Most of you are somewhere along the spectrum between 0% and 100% self-discipline and self-care at all times. You probably participate in at least a few self-sabotaging behaviors.

To stop hurting yourself is to treat yourself with a little more kindness and self-respect, to set aside unwise and unhealthy habits, and implement in their place more healthy and constructive ones.

Everything you do registers. Everything has impact. All causes have effects, all effects have causes. Every thought, feeling, word and action is a cause set in motion. You may not be able to escape the consequences of your actions. Thus, it is wise to be mindful of all you do.

Take care of yourself on all levels.
Take care of your body, mind, heart and spirit.
Tend to your relationships and your finances.

Exercise your body and your mind. Be mindful of how every behavior hurts you or helps you. Food is medicine, or poison. Have a practice, and practice, practice, practice. How you practice is how you play. Your life is your practice, so practice every day. Lay solid foundations in your life. Lay the groundwork for what you wish to build. Honor the process. Take action today. Do not delay. And finish what you start.

Cultivate self-awareness. Shed light on what is in the dark. Get to know your blind spots. Know your traumas, and stop passing them on. Confront and heal your pain. Learn to regulate your nervous system so you can stay present with your triggers, and transform unconscious reactivity into conscious responsiveness. Take control of your mind and emotions. Take control of your responses and behaviors. Take control of yourself and your life. Model this behavior for other people.

Take control of your thoughts, feelings, words and actions. Every behavior has consequences, subtle or significant. Be your own master, create your own physical health, mental health, emotional health, financial prosperity and security, fulfilling interpersonal relationships, joyful romance and love, authentic creative self-expression, meaningful contributions to this world, and a sound connection with Source.

Also recruit the help of others in supporting you, since you are a pack animal.

Live with integrity. Come into alignment with yourself. Align your actions with your words. Show me what you can do, don't tell me. Keep your agreements. Develop a trustworthy character.

Remember the primary importance of connection. Remember that, in relation to other people, everything you do creates greater connection or separation. Give people the gift of being seen and heard, the gift of validation. Allow people to be who they are. Grant everyone a wide berth. Practice discernment of other people's characters. Find those with whom you resonate, so you can surround yourself with the right people, and find your tribe. Practice compassion from a distance for those you do not wish to allow into your life.

Most life lessons come down to taking care of yourself and interacting skillfully with other people.

There are countless more lessons not included in this book, yet this feels like a good place to finish, ending where the journey began.

Today, stop hurting yourself. Start taking care of yourself. Wherever you are at on the spectrum of self-care versus self-destruction, just move one step closer towards self-care. Choose one thing to nurture yourself today. Then do it. Make this a habit every day.

For more life lessons visit www.365lifelessons.com, where you can sign up to receive one simple and practical life lesson every day.

What one thing will you do today, to stop hurting yourself, and start taking care of yourself?

OPPOSITE

There are no opposites to this life lesson that will serve you well. Stop hurting yourself. Start taking care of yourself. Good luck out there!

ABOUT THE AUTHOR

Isaac Freed was born in San Francisco, California, the son and grandson of immigrants and war refugees.

From the outside, his formative years may appear benign. Yet, subjectively, when unfortunate things happened to him, he took them personally, causing him to be very unhappy, and leading him down the parallel paths of self-destruction and self-discovery. Perhaps he brought his past lives with him, as his parents say he was born angry. Ultimately, all this has resulted in the collection of books he has authored, including this one.

While far from perfect, and still striving to embody all of the wisdom in this book, he has made some progress in developing self-awareness and an understanding of how to relate constructively to others.

Book number one, <u>How To Not Give A Fuck In Ten Easy Steps</u>, was an accidental inspiration that turned out to be a book about awareness and compassion, a personal growth guide with a Buddhist inclination. While it is a reflection of his own journey towards greater self-realization, readers have commented on the immense value his wisdom and insight, delivered with wit and simplicity, have provided them in their own lives.

His second book, <u>99 Life Lessons That I Learned The Hard Way So You Don't Have To</u>, is a continuation of the journey towards greater awareness of self and others. It is a collection of practical concepts to cultivate fulfilling relationships with one's self, other people and the world at large, that can be applied day by day, one step at a time. Isaac's current mission (as of 2023) is to implement and practice embodying the lessons in this book, and share the messages with others who are open and ready to receive them.

About The Author

In addition to collecting and disseminating meaningful life lessons, Isaac enjoys the great outdoors, laughing, physical exercise, growing food, preparing and sharing delicious meals, listening to and playing music, going to the beach, building fires, time alone and quality time with other people. His favorite things to do include eating fresh fruit, swimming in the ocean, snowboarding, wine tasting and laughing while making love.

You can read his short essays at www.isaacfreed.com, and sign up for 365 Life Lessons, where you will receive one simple and practical life lesson every day that you can easily apply in your life.

www.365lifelessons.com

STAY CONNECTED

Thank you for reading this book. My wish is that you can apply the lessons presented here, share them with other people, and add substance, meaning and fulfillment to your life.

To continue on this path, you can enjoy receiving one short, sweet life lesson every day of the year, upon which to reflect, and to implement in your life, for the cost of one cup of coffee every month:

<u>www.365lifelessons.com</u>

Isaac Freed

Made in the USA
Middletown, DE
03 August 2023

36154318R00179